MW00355653

Like the Prodigal Son I Returned

Steven "Red" Salas

ISBN 978-1-64349-995-6 (paperback)
ISBN 978-1-64416-197-5 (hardcover)
ISBN 978-1-64349-996-3 (digital)

Copyright © 2018 by Steven "Red" Salas

All rights reserved. No part of this publication may be reproduced, distributed, or transmitted in any form or by any means, including photocopying, recording, or other electronic or mechanical methods without the prior written permission of the publisher. For permission requests, solicit the publisher via the address below.

Christian Faith Publishing, Inc.
832 Park Avenue
Meadville, PA 16335
www.christianfaithpublishing.com

The events of this book are true; characters' names have been changed to protect their identities.

Printed in the United States of America

For Manuel C. Salas Sr., the dad G-d Almighty
blessed me with. I miss you every day.
And Daniel David Chandler, my first good
friend when I came to San Antonio.
Rest easy, my friend.

As you read this book you might notice that I write G-o-d as "G-d". Some of you might be wondering what this is about. The reason is simple; it is a sign of respect. This is a Jewish custom that I follow. "Jews do not casually write any Name of G-o-d.... Judaism does not prohibit writing the Name of G-o-d per se; it prohibits only erasing or defacing a Name of G-o-d. However, observant Jews avoid writing any Name of God casually because of the risk that the written Name might later be defaced, obliterated or destroyed accidentally or by one who does not know better. Normally, They avoid writing the Name by substituting letters or syllables, for example, writing "G-d" instead of "G-o-d." When I write it and you read it. You know exactly what I'm saying, even though I haven't actually written his name out.

No, I'm not of the Jewish faith, I am a Christian. I recently did a DNA test. The results say I have 2% Jewish Diaspora. That has nothing to do with it. But I do agree with their custom show of respect. Therefore I choose to do the same.

I would like to thank the following
My creator G-d Almighty for his Son Jesus.
My wife Diane. She is my soul mate. A very strong woman. She is an answer to a prayer. I just didn't know it at the time.
Jim Cohn my spiritual mentor and good friend Who I always learn something from about the Lord. A friend I can always call on and he will listen and pray for me.
Ashley Loewe, who I consider my friend. Her and her husband Ross. She helped me put together my summery.

Chapter 1

Jeremiah 1:5 "Before I formed you in the womb I knew you, before you were born I set you apart."

Growing up in Southeastern Wisconsin is just about different as any other place. I was born June 4, 1966. I never knew ninety days prior to the date before I was born, an American subculture was also born. Even more bizarre, I would become a part of it.

I lived in a town called Racine. Its name comes from the French word for *root*. It was named by a party of French explorers as they entered the mouth of the Root River, which runs through various areas of the city. Native American–occupied Racine as far back as 10,000 BC. There is a cemetery called Mound Cemetery. It has Indian burial mounds that date back to 500 BC. Racine was settled by Captain Gilbert Knapp of Chatham, Massachusetts. He had explored the area in 1818, returning later with financial backing in 1834.

It's a favorite spot for anglers in the fall as trout and salmon go up the river to change color and spawn. After completing their mission, they die. As a boy, I would try my luck and skill at trying to catch one. I had a cheap Zebco 404. It was the fishing rod to have in that day. I would bungee my tackle box and fishing rod to my handlebars. I'd set out on the bike I made out of parts I got from the trash. I had to get to the river and get in on the action. Catching one would give you bragging rights with other kids. We would all compare our catches to see who caught the biggest. I think it starts with men when we are boys. There would always be a kid that had the story of the big one that got away.

All along the banks of the Root River, you would see young and old, everyone fishing. Tackle boxes alongside lawn chairs. Cigarettes hanging out of some people's mouth as they waited in anticipation for a fish to strike their line.

Racine is a diverse small Midwest city with a large Danish population. The eastern part of the city is on the shore of Lake Michigan. To give you some idea about Wisconsin itself, Minnesota borders it to the west and part of Iowa and Illinois to the south and Canada is to the north. It's the home of William Horlick, the inventor of malted milk. It's an industrial town. Some of the factories it included at the time when I was young was J. I. Case, Massey Ferguson, Jacobson, SC Johnson Wax, Modine, and Dremel. For the most part, it was a nice small city at that time.

Work became scarce in the '80s. Many people were laid off or let go because of cutbacks and the economy. Unless you knew someone, it was hard to get a decent job to support yourself and a small family. Fast-food joints were plentiful even back then. Honestly, I think the fast-food boom may have started around the late '70s in Southeastern Wisconsin. I don't know for sure. It sure seemed like they started popping up a lot.

Summers are short and winters seemed long and very cold. But no matter what the weather is like when you're a kid, you always find something fun to do. Building snow forts, tobogganing, sledding, and riding aluminum saucers down hills or developed and designated areas provided by the Department of Parks and Recreation.

Building snowmen and having snowball fights were something you did while waiting to be picked up by your friends' parents. It seemed I could always catch a ride home after sledding. Occasionally, I would be told by my friend's parents that they couldn't give me a ride because they were going somewhere before they went home. I'd find myself alone walking. Not being able to make it home before dark. I would walk on the sidewalks that sparkled like gems from a thin layer of snow. Walking down Washington Avenue past the Capitol Movie Theater. Looking into the entrance, noticing the bored usher standing with one hand supporting his slouching head. Crossing an intersection past Durangos Pizza Parlor where my dad would take me to eat. Passing Nelson's Dime Store where you could buy penny candy and balsa wood gliders.

As it grew darker and darker, I'd gaze up into the dark sky and wonder about G-d. I always felt he loved me and I always felt he was watching over me. I would bring my head down again toward my path on the sidewalk. Snowflakes would be floating diagonally past a bright street light and blending into the ground or snow bank then disappearing in seconds as I continued my walk home. Passing all the nice houses. The fire house on the corner of Washington and Lathrop Avenues. The Loom of Demark furniture store. Finally making it to Oregon Street. The Mortensens lived on the corner of Washington and Oregon Streets. They had a nice home with weeping willow trees in their yard. As dark as it was, it looked to be after midnight. The streets were quiet; nobody was driving or walking on them but me. Finally I would make it to 1234 Oregon Street where I lived.

I grew up in the '70s while the good things of yesteryear still existed. The drive-in theater, soda in glass bottles, gasoline under one dollar, and new color TVs if your family could afford one.

I would ride my bike around my neighborhood with baseball cards in the spokes of my bicycle wheels to make it sound like a motorcycle. I would ride around with no shirt on, wearing Tough Skin jeans from Sears and Chuck Taylor Converse high-top basketball shoes.

Most kids would have gotten into trouble had their mothers known we were taking their clothespins off the clothesline, but if you only took a couple, they wouldn't miss them. They were the pinch clothespins the kept the cards attached to the forks on the bike while the baseball cards rattled like a motor in the spokes of the wheels. I'd pretend I was riding a big Harley Davidson.

The Harley Davidson motorcycle factory was in Milwaukee. Racine was only about thirty miles south from Milwaukee. I would see the chopped Harleys riding around my neighborhood. The wild-looking operators of these chromed-out machines would have long messy hair, big beards like Vikings, oil-stained and holey jeans, faded Harley shirts, black beat-up and scuffed boots, and tattoos all over their bodies. They rode at high speed like daredevils. My friends and I would watch these outcasts of society, covering our ears to muffle the sound of the exhaust pipes as they cracked out their throttles as they passed us.

Home life wasn't a pleasant place for me to be. My mother was always screaming about something. She never seemed happy. Everything bothered her. Profanity, sarcasm, and being abrasive were her trademarks. Rarely was I given motherly love. Nurturing was not something she gave me often. A few times at all that I can remember.

My dad was complete opposite. He never raised his voice or used profanity or acted vulgar. He was a kind, loving, gentle soul. Always good to me. Always playing with me. Picking me up and throwing me in the air. He would played catch with me with baseball gloves that he bought me and my brother.

My mother and father divorced when I was six. I only had one brother and no sisters and my brother was the oldest. He would sleep in longer than I would. One thing that is the same today and I'm sure will be the same in the future is most young kids get up early and eat a bowl of cold cereal in front of the TV on Saturday and Sunday to watch the morning cartoons. The good cartoons: Bugs Bunny, Popeye the Sailor, and the rest of the Warner Brother characters.

I was no different in that aspect. I did get up a lot earlier than most kids. Prior to 6:00 a.m., there were no cartoons on yet. The only thing to choose from were different church programs. I always remember watching church on TV; Rex Humbard is one TV evangelist I recall watching. Billy Graham would have specials from time to time. Church would come on before cartoons started at 7:00 a.m.

As far back as I can remember, G-d's Holy Spirit has always tugged at the strings of my heart and soul. His spirit always told me there was more to him than what I was being told at home. What I was being taught was Catholicism. I would listen attentively to the TV preacher as he preached the gospel. I would hear about the love of G-d and salvation through Jesus Christ.

I was raised in a Catholic home. My mother and father kept the tradition of each of their families that had been passed down from generation to generations. My dad didn't go to Catholic church often. My mother would go to Holy Name Catholic Church close to Lake Michigan.

I never got into trouble for watching those church programs even though they always contradicted what my family was trying to teach me about G-d and Jesus.

My mother would take my brother and me to attended mass from time to time. Mostly Christmas and Easter. Midnight mass was torture trying to stay awake through the whole service. Sometimes I couldn't help it, I would dose off, only to be awakened by my mother grabbing the skin of my arm and twisting it with her long fingernails. The pain would shoot through me like electricity and I would sit up like a good Catholic was supposed to.

You always hear of how mean Catholic nuns were supposed to be. If in fact it was true, I really don't know. My mother could have been a substitute nun if it was true. My memory goes back as I can remember. She seemed like she hated me. How you might ask? She's a mother. Well, I can't answer that. I just never felt loved.

I would look in her direction only to be met by her dagger piercing stare. It was the stare that I recognized as I had better pay attention.

As much as I tried to pay attention to the priest as he babbled on about something or another, I couldn't follow along. It was nothing as interesting as the TV preachers.

We would constantly stand, kneel, and stand again. Make the sign of the cross and repeat whatever the priest would tell us to repeat. It never made any sense to me. But I'd followed along as the family members of the many generations back hundreds and hundreds of years to Valladolid, Spain, did before me. Where the Salas name began.

I became an altar boy. It wasn't my idea. It was my mother's idea. I could have cared less one way or another. She would be able to brag to her friends that my brother and I were both in service to the Catholic church. Her friends would exalt her and say, "Oh, you must be so proud." Which she was eagerly to except and savor the flavor of the verbal pats on her back. Matthew 23:12 says, "For those who exalt themselves will be humbled, and those who humble themselves will be exalted."

My mother always portrayed herself as being sanctified; we had large statues in different areas in the house. These statures were images of Catholic saints. Exodus 20:4 says, "Thou shalt not make unto thee graven images."

There were candles burning in front of each of them. Those candles were never supposed to go out, nor was I supposed to go near them. There would be severe consequences if I disobeyed the strict rules that my mother made and enforced like a Gestapo chief.

My mother was a short overweight woman who was constantly full of anger. I don't know what had happened to her in life to make her so bitter. She would get upset for the littlest things and yell. Unless you drove her to the point of her beating you. The beatings I endured were just that. Beatings not spankings. They were not meant for discipline. They were meant to inflict pain. There is a difference in a spanking and a beating. She would whip us with a wooden paddle with malice. At least, it felt like that. Even the look on her face when she was administering a severe corporal punishment was that of hate.

There were no child abuse laws like the ones that exist today. Depending on the offense, I would be screamed at, slapped in the face, paddled, or sometimes made to kneel on uncooked rice.

She rarely embraced me or showed me much of any other forms of affection. You would think that all mothers are the same. You might figure that because they carried you in their own body that they would have the mother-child bond. Most woman do, but not all of them. Mine was one of the ones who didn't

I was constantly castigated for loving my father. She would scream and say, "Shut the f—— up, your father is a no-good piece of s—— and you're worthless piece of s—— like him. He was whoring around on me until one day I threw him out."

Her way was it. You had better agree with what she was saying if you knew what was good for you. She always had her way of doing everything, no matter what you thought or had the courage to say. I would stay quiet most of the time, not agreeing with her and certainly not disagreeing.

If you took her side and showed total allegiance to her and her beliefs, you would be fine. My brother was an easy sellout. He would tell on me and repeat whatever my father might say during his visitation with us. It would earn him love and affection from her.

Like an informant wearing a wiretap in his brain, filing all my dad would say. Saving it for rewards of love and appreciation or sometimes if he wanted things from the store. Items that we rarely received. You know a cheap toy or a snack of some sort. He would also wait until she erupted like a volcano, then use it like a Monopoly get-out-of-jail-free card. He bring up our visitation and reveal valuable intel to her.

I would not conform to her way. I resisted. Not like Mahatma Gandhi or Martin Luther King, but more like the Great Apache Chief Geronimo. In my young mind, I resisted. I would tell myself my dad isn't a bad person, she is. One day, I'm going to get bigger, and she won't be able to hit or hurt me anymore. One day, things will be better, Lord, I just know it. The preachers would say it on TV and I believed it.

I would say, "One day, Lord Jesus, I'm going to get me a job as garbage man and make money and move away from this horrible place. Better yet, I'll become a soldier and go to a far-off distant land where she will never find me."

The dreams of a little boy who had nobody but Jesus. Alienated in the place that was supposed to be my home. A home maybe for my mother and brother, yes, but not for me. For me, it was where I laid my head at night. Like a homeless person who sometimes knows no other place but one doorway or alley. One where they'd feel a little comfortable only after drifting off into REM sleep. Finding peace for a few hours.

I never have been a person that did well with rules either. Don't get me wrong, I mean with corrupt totalitarian rules. Had I been born Jewish in the time of Moses or in Nazi Germany, I would have surely been executed by my oppressors. I don't know where that driving force of resistance came from, but it still exists in me today. If I see someone being treated unjustly, I involve myself.

Psalms 82:3–4 says, "Stand up for the weak and for children whose fathers have died. Protect the rights of people who are poor or treated badly. Save those who are weak and needy. Save them from the power of sinful people."

So I survived many years of abuse at the hands of whom I knew to be my mother the best I could.

I would lie on the bottom of the bunk beds that my brother and I would share. I would meditate on G-d and say, "I know one day, Lord, you will make everything right."

I would look out the bedroom window out at the glistering stars and the bright moon. The sounds of crickets chirping, an occasional bark from a neighbor's dog and my brother's heavy breathing as he was in a deep sleep. All the different sounds would finally make me fall asleep also.

I drifted off into another world. Where I was part of a real family. Where the mother was thin and pretty. She had on lipstick, pearl earrings, wore a pretty dress and fancy shoes. Where the dinners were more like feasts. The dinner table was arranged perfect. The dream mother would stroke my hair into place as she made sure the family had everything they needed before she took her seat. Where the perfect mother of my dreams later that evening would pull the covers up to my neck at bedtime as she simultaneously kissed me gently on my cheek, making me feel like I was loved.

Oh yes, a real family, it felt so good. It was the kind of dreams that felt so good, you never wanted to wake up. If I could only stay in my dreams.

Chapter 2

I was suddenly awakened and realized I was only dreaming. Like the country Western song lyrics of a song my dad used to play. And then I woke up and looked around me at the four gray walls that surrounded me and I realized I was only dreaming. The echoes of my mother's voice yelling, "Steven, if I have to come in there, I'm going to yank you out of that bed and whip you're a—— good."

She meant it. The school week always began the same way I would jump from my bed like a recruit in basic training. I would dress myself like a fireman who had just heard the fire alarm in the station house.

I'd tuck my short-sleeved plaid button shirt into my jeans, throw on my Converse high tops, and high-tail it to the kitchen. Hoping my belt was right. Hoping my shirt was tucked in right. Hoping my hair wasn't out of place. Maybe today would be the day. Maybe today she'd love me. She didn't have to lose weight or wear fancy shoes and jewelry. Her love is all I really wanted. For her to accept me. To let me be part of their inner circle. I'd pour my cereal and milk while she was barking orders at me not to spill the milk because I was in a hurry.

Soon after I gobbled down my Kellogg's cornflakes, we were rushing out the door and into her big old Ford LTD four-door. As the big old boat backed up and then down, the snow-covered incline of our gravel driveway that was hidden by the newly fallen snow. We would slide crooked from the rubber against the slippery snow and then straight again into the street we lived on. Like a christened ship that reached water free from port, our travel began.

Shortly after, we would pull into the cul-de-sac at the rear of Giese Elementary. There was a long flight of stairs that led to the back of our school. I would rush out of the car like soldiers unloading from a cattle car in Fort Leonardwood, Missouri.

My mother would pull away, and when I saw her car drive far enough away, I would walk to my class. School was a great getaway for me. I could relax and enjoy the company of other kids and the teachers. My teachers were always kind to me. They would squat down to my level and put their arm around me. Always smiling, always sweet. They were thin and pretty, like the mother in my dreams. Sometimes, I would pretend that the teacher was my mom and I had a good life.

I never did well in school. A few times, I was sure I wouldn't pass to the next grade. That no kid left behind thing wasn't around when I was a kid. You either did well or you were held back to repeat the grade again. I just didn't seem to get what all the other kids were learning. I didn't understand the curriculum the teachers were trying to explain. Maybe I was more interested in the small bit of affection I construed my teacher was giving me.

Have you ever heard the saying, "All good things come to an end"? Well, they do. Like I said school was my getaway.

The clock would eventually reach three p.m. and school was out for the day. I'd grab my cheap winter jacket from K-mart and begin my trek home. Back to the concentration camp I went. Never walking with my brother, he was always with his friends, and they didn't like me or want me around them. I would pass and look at all the beautiful houses and shiny new cars. Drifting thoughts of pretending that I lived there and a Mrs. Clever type of mother anticipated my arrival home.

Block after block until I reached my street. Down the steep hill to the middle of the block and up the driveway of 1234 Oregon Street. I'd open my winter jacket, reach inside my undershirt, and pull out the chrome-beaded chain, the kind you get on a rabbit's foot key chain, only longer. I would finally reach the end of it where my blue house key was at. Working it into the lock with one hand, trying to hold the doorknob with the other hand and keep my metal lunch pail between my knees all at the same time.

I would go inside and turn on the TV and wait for Batman and Robin to come on. The original Batman and Robin (Adam West and Burt Ward). I recall sitting with my brother in front of our TV. As the intro to the series would come on and it would say Batman in color. I would say to my brother, "I don't know why they always say that, it's never in color." He would tell me to shut up. He would say, "You are always saying that." He would try to adjust the rabbit ear antenna to get a better reception. He then would return to his seat to watch the episode.

It never dawned on me when I was a boy. It was because we had a black and white TV. That was the reason it was never in color. Watching the clocks every move, knowing my mother was en route to the house. When you want the clock to move fast, it never does. You look at it and it seems like it only moved five or six minutes. When my mother was coming home, the clock always moved fast, it seemed.

Soon after the programs we liked to watch ended, my mother's car would come up the drive and pass the living room window. I knew what was coming. She would throw her purse and jacket in the kitchen chair. She'd walk across back and forth on the worn and torn linoleum floor and begin cooking our dinner. Complaining and mumbling under her breath. That was better than her screaming for no reason. There weren't many days like that. Most days, she would come in screaming like a Gestapo, "Achtung, Achtung," as I hurried to carry out her commands. She should have just said, "I have vays to make you learn, Steven, und I vill enjoy teaching you each and every vun of them." Meaning if you don't get with my program, I'll beat it into you.

Wednesdays were always something to look forward to. It was visitation with my dad. He was so good to me and my brother. My dad was from Texas. He was born in a small town named Millet. It's an unincorporated town about seventy-five miles south of San Antonio. He left home after he graduating from high school. He came to Racine because there were lots of good jobs. My dad had a hard life. His dad had been hit and killed by a train when he was four years old. My grandmother raised him, his older brother, and his four sisters by cleaning farmhouses, washing laundry on a scrub board for some, and also ironing for locals of their very small community. My dad and his siblings would help my grandmother by picking cotton and working the farm fields in the sweltering Texas summers when school was out. My dad said his mother couldn't read or write. She only spoke Spanish and that he and his siblings taught her how to write her name. It's all she could write. He said she made sure that all six of them graduated high school. That she wanted them to have an education.

Once I remember my mom telling me that my dad's mother was stupid because she could not speak English, read, or write. I told my dad what she said. He told me to tell her that she may not have been able to speak English. She may not know how to read and write, but she made sure all six of her children graduated high school. He said your mother's mom can speak English and Spanish. She can read and write also. And your mom and her four siblings; none of them graduated high school. He was very protective of his mother.

My dad wasn't very affectionate to me. He never hugged or kissed me. He never even said he loved me very many times that I remember, but I knew he did. Actions speak louder than words like they say.

He would spend quality time with us. We would sit together me, my brother and him and be waited on at Durango's Italian restaurant. The old Italian proprietor, Mr. Durango, would toss the pizza dough into the air, shaping it like his ancestors did generations before him. With his heavy Italian accent, thin medium frame with silver hair, I would hear him calling to the waitress, "Maria, there-sa cutomers they just-a come-a in."

I would sit next to my dad and he would ask me how I was doing in school. I would smile, saying, "I'm doing great, Dad."

I was lying to him, but I wanted him to be happy. I wanted to impress him. I wanted to matter to someone. After all, nobody ever asked me question about anything but my dad. He was always very good to me. I heard it said somewhere, there are people who really love you a lot, they just don't know how to say it.

It was the same way as G-d. I never heard him say it to me, but I knew he loved me too. I felt it in my young heart.

Now my brother would sit there quietly with us. He was waiting to gather intel for my mother. Never getting involved in our conversations much. He would sip on his orange crush soda through a red-striped white straw that was in the neck of the glass bottle. If my dad would ask him anything, he had few words; his allegiance was to my mother. He had to get information for him to stay on her good side.

The evening would come to an end quickly, and we would have to go back home. Back to the same old routine as before.

There were different activities going on in school like Cub Scouts. I wasn't allowed to be involved with anything. It was either too much or we didn't have enough money for me to do anything.

I would watch as other kids my age would participate in different functions and activities. I would wonder what it was like and what would they do at the functions while walking past the gymnasium.

My brother was a Cub Scout and my mom was even a den mother. I remember the Steinberg family from my childhood. One of the sons was in the pack my mother was running. He must have come once or twice and then never returned. After I got older, I thought it may have been all the statues and candles in the house. I thought he may have mentioned it at home and his father wouldn't let him return. The Steinberg family were Jewish. I didn't have any knowledge of the difference between the beliefs of Jews and Christians. Not as a boy. As a boy, I didn't even know Jesus was the manifestation of the Holy Ghost in the flesh. Let alone idol worship. I was being indoctrinated with Catholicism. The propaganda contrary to the Holy Scriptures.

One day, a school friend of mine named Scott was telling me about the Boy Scouts. He said I should join. I told him my mom wouldn't let me. I kept on explaining to him it wasn't possible. It just wouldn't happen. I know I've been through this a million times. In my mind, I would say, "You don't know that my mom hates me and it gave her pleasure to tell me no."

He was so persistent that he finally persuaded me to ask her. He went with me, and when I asked my mom, she said like usual, we didn't have the money for the uniform. Scott interjected by saying,

"Mrs. Salas, Steve can have my brother's uniform, he's not in scouting anymore."

My mom said, "Would your mother be all right with giving it to Steven?"

He said, "Yes, ma'am."

I don't recall him even asking her, but who cares? I was one step closer to being able to do something I saw other boys doing.

With her hands on her wide hips and silent for a moment, she said yes. I guess so. That will fine. I thought I was imagining what I heard her say. I was so excited. I couldn't believe she actually said yes. Was I dreaming? No, I wasn't.

That night, I went to bed with a big smile on my face. I must have dreamed of camping out and learning the ways of the outdoors. Earning merit badges. Yeah, merit badges coving my chest, something that would bring me compliments. Pats on the backs. People would ask me of what each badge represented. Look at me, I'm important. I matter. I'm somebody. Never realizing I was somebody already. Somebody worth dying for. That's right, I was somebody to Jesus Christ. Always watching over me and directing my path.

Romans 5:8 says, "But G-d demonstrates his own love for us in this: While we were still sinners, Christ died for us."

In the next couple of days, Scott and his dad came to pick me up, and off we went to the Boy Scout meeting. I remember it was in the banquet hall of a big Lutheran church near the intersection of Lathrop and Washington Avenues across from the fire house. The same one I would walk past sometimes. It was in the west side area of the city.

I went inside with a big smile on my face as Scott showed me around and introduced me to everyone. He even introduced me to the Boy Scout leader. I extended my hand with a smile from ear to ear. He asked me a few different questions: what school I attended, what grade I was in, and how old I was. Occasionally, I would look away and admire the other boys in their uniforms with different color badges sewed to the shirt. Then turn my attention back to the scout leader, answering his questions with "Yes, sir."

That evening was so good. We had snacks and did different fun activities. Ten or twenty minutes before the Boy Scout meeting ended, the group leader asked to talk to me in the hall. I complied eagerly. When we got in the hall of the church by ourselves, the Boy Scout leader squatted down to eye level with me and said Steve, "You're only ten years old. You have to wait a few more years. There are age requirements we go by."

My smile left my face as my lip began to tremble. As the tears rolled down my face, I said, "No, please, you don't understand. She never lets me do anything. Please, sir, please, she never lets me do anything."

He said, "I'm sorry, Steve, those are the rules."

As he walked away, I slowly slid down against the wall and down until I rested on the back of my Converse basketball high-top shoes and cried.

I failed again. I almost made it this time. I thought I was in for sure. As her words came back to me again, "You'll never amount to anything," I began to think maybe she's right. I was just a loser. I was never meant to win. I don't know why, but I don't remember anything hurting my feelings as bad as that did as a boy. It was the saddest time of my life to this day. Even as a man, I don't think anything ever hurt my feelings that bad.

Chapter 3

Psalm 100:5 "For the LORD is good and his love endures forever; his faithfulness continues through all generations."

As time moves on, everyone gets older. Somehow or another, I ended up living with my dad off and on. It wasn't very long and we never really got around to bonding with each other as a father and son would. With the divorce of my mother and father when I was six years old didn't give me an opportunity to be with my dad the way other boys were. Believe it or not, divorce wasn't that common back then. I don't recall any of my classmates or neighborhood friend's parents being divorced. That made me feel even more like an outcast.

I'd would insightfully notice how my life was quite different from other boys and girls I went to school with. My clothes weren't as good. My house wasn't as nice. I had a piece of junk bike and they had shiny new ones.

Before I knew it, I was thirteen years old. Thirteen I think. My life hadn't change much other than I had gotten older. I started to notice girls more, that's one thing that changed. I had my crushes on girls like every other boy that was my age. I spent a lot of time wandering here and there. Neighborhood parks, strip malls, and sometimes K-mart. My dad would give me money so while he was at work, I could go get a submarine sandwich at K-mart for lunch. I would ride my bike all over town.

During the summer, I was at his house alone or my stepmom Annette was there sometimes. I was very mean to Annette. I was very disrespectful to her. She was always very nice to my brother and me. I was defiant. She was willing to give me the motherly love I so desperately wanted and needed, but I rejected it from her. Thinking I just wanted my mother to love me the way I loved her, but I knew she never would. It may have been different had I given Annette a chance to be a mother to me. I'm ashamed today the way I treated her. I know many times I hurt her feelings. I should have never treated her that way. I'm very sorry and hope that she forgives me.

Once I was disrespecting Annette to the point my dad had to step in. He grabbed me by the arm and took me into my room. He sat me on my bed then sat next to me. He said, "Steven, I know why you're so angry."

I said, "I'm not angry, Dad."

He said, "Inside, son, inside."

Again I said no. My dad was a very calm man. Never swore, hardly ever lost his temper. He said, "You're so full of anger deep inside because you just want your mother to love you. Well, she's never going to. She's not right in the head."

My eyes started to well up. Tears started to run down my face. As I cried, I said, "You don't know nothing, Dad."

I placed my face in both of my hands and cried. My dad put both of his arms around my skinny frame and hugged me. He said, "I love you, mi hijo (Spanish for "my son"). I'll always love you."

He said this to me then walked out of my room. I sat there lost in my thoughts. I regained my composure. I also left my bedroom and headed outside. Out into my neighborhood and to roam the streets.

As I ran and wandered like a stray dog who had just broken his chain. I found myself in trouble with the law. Mostly petty crimes, shoplifting, stealing bikes, and fighting. A few times in front of a juvenile judge and that was all it took. My mom kind of just let my dad keep me because I had become quite rebellious and ran off from her a few times in the past. It was the easier way out for her. She didn't want to burden herself; it wasn't profitable to her. It only mattered if she could have total control over someone.

You know G-d's unconditional love never fails. I believe that he had always been looking down on me. I was trying to fulfill my sinful nature that had been passed down to me from the time of Adam. G-d's love and mercy seen me through everything all the time. Even to this very day he continues to see me through my life's obstacles.

Psalm 100:5 says, "For the LORD is good and his love endures forever; his faithfulness continues through all generations."

Romans 5:8 says, "But G-d demonstrates his own love for us in this: While we were still sinners, Christ died for us."

I can truly say that I have experienced this love that is described in both of those scriptures. Our G-d is a perfect G-d and he doesn't ever make mistakes. He was merciful. The court eventfully ordered me to live foster care for my own good and welfare. They felt that with my dad working all the time I didn't have the supervision I needed.

Never under estimate the G-d of Israel. The G-d of Abraham, Isaac, and Jacob has a plan for everything and everybody. This was only the beginning of myself witnessing the great mystery of G-d. The mystery that G-d will reveal to anyone who has an open heart to receive it. I've met and spoken to so many people in my life. Some who know what I'm talking about and some who don't. There are even some I've met who refuse to believe that G-d exists. If you will just open your heart and receive G-d's blessing, you will be amazed at how good your life could be. You would be surprised at how much G-d wants to do in your life, if only you would be willing to let him.

Most people live day to day never experiencing the love G-d has for them. Not because he refuses to love them, but because they refuse his love. He is always there waiting on us as individuals. Never forcing himself on us, only waiting for the day we want to receive the love of his only begotten son Jesus Christ.

Chapter 4

It was a long slow ride to Union Grove, Wisconsin. The month and year is vague to me. I do remember as we approach the city limits of Racine. We were traveling by automobile, me and a female social worker from the Racine County Court. Arrangements had been made and I was to be placed with a family.

I never left Racine County, but when you're a fifteen-year-old boy out of your neighborhood, it seems like you crossed the world.

Union Grove is a small town west of Racine. It has lots of farms and farm fields. Rows and rows of cabbage in the fields zipped passed me. I'd try to focus my eyes and look down a single row of cabbage as we flew past them. Never being able to do it. I eventually just turned away and looked thought the front windshield from the back seat where I was sitting. I leaned against the door, wishing I was not having to go where I was going. As we drew closer and closer to our final destination, I would doze off and then open my eyes again. Never really falling completely asleep.

We turned off the Highway 20 and made turns that I don't remember. I do remember the last turn. It was a right turn off the pavement and onto a very long gravel road. As we approached the aluminum-sided two-story house that was painted white with dark trim, I could see what appeared to be movement in the house. The four-door sedan's tires crackled as it rolled over the number 1 limestone in the driveway of the property. The car finally came to a halt near the front door of the house. I grabbed my bag of what clothes I had and followed the social worker to the front door as instructed.

She gave a few taps on the door frame and waited. I could hear footsteps approach the door way from the inside. The door swiftly opened, and there stood a young man about my age. He seemed very content and, with a smile, asked us to come in. All three of us climbed a very small flight of stairs. At the top and to the left was the living room with a TV on. A gentleman in his midfifties was watching the TV but moved his attention toward our direction as his peripheral vision had picked up our presence. With a Spanish accent, he said, "Come in," in a very hospitable manner. The way where you knew his words were from the heart. Mr. Romo was a medium-sized thin man who wore button dress shirts casually and slacks. His sleeves were sometimes rolled up just below his elbows. He had dark eyes with a full but thin mustache that appeared to be groomed that way on purpose. His hair was combed neatly to the side. Maybe it stayed in place with Tres Flores Brilliantine.

A Hispanic lady came out of the kitchen; her smile was from ear to ear, welcoming us also. Mrs. Romo wore women's slacks and a blouse. But her smile was radiant. The love of Jesus Christ shined out of them both. We all got acquainted around their dining room table. I sat mostly with my head hung down. Not wanting to be where the court had ordered me to be.

The young man who answered the door was introduced to me as Messala. He looked Mediterranean with olive-colored skin, well-groomed, wearing nice clothes, and very well-mannered. He extended his had to me as a gesture of his friendship. I felt as if I were in the twilight zone. I imagined Rod Serling was going to pop out anytime to narrate my life story.

Why were these people so kind and happy? Nobody ever smiled that much at me or welcomed me the way they did.

Nevertheless, there was no mistaking their love and kindness was real. I wasn't used to a woman as a mother figure treating me like I was loved. So I reached for Messala's extended hand. Not wanting to offend him. Because he hadn't done anything wrong to me.

The social worked completed the necessary forms required by the court and she said goodbye to the Mr. and Mrs. Romo, Messala, and me. From the large living room widows that were fogged along the edges from the cold outside, I watched her car slowly drive back down the gravel driveway we had driven up thirty minutes prior.

The car made a left turn onto the farm road again. Pieces of the car's silhouette were barely visible through the overgrown weeds of the shoulder of the road. This was it. *I was here for good,* I thought.

Messala was instructed to show me where my sleeping quarters would be. We shared a room in the lower level of the house. Messala made small talk with me try to get me to loosen up and feel at home. No matter what he said or tried to do I was depressed and was I so ever homesick. I stayed awake that night, thinking back when I was real young a little boy. Thinking of my time in prayer with the Lord. The feeling of guilt. It was because I was created in G-d's image. That's the reason I felt so bad. My flesh had rebelled against my spirit. The spirit the wanted me to do G-d's will. I tossed and turned all night long. That first night I didn't get very much sleep.

The following morning took so long to come being that I couldn't fall asleep. I though again and again how I followed the desires of my flesh which is just what the enemy wanted me to do. After I was placed in foster care, the devil laughed at me because he had ruined my life at that point. It seemed by the time I finally did fall asleep, I heard the movement throughout the house. It was an indication to me that it was time to get up and moving. The smell of fresh brewing coffee confirmed it. Everything was peaceful in this house. No yelling or slamming things around as my biological mother would do.

I followed Messala up the two flights of stairs that led to the Romo's living room. I was greeted by the radiant smile of Mrs. Romo once again. She was preparing breakfast. She said good morning to me and Messala. I mumbled back, "Good morning," in a depressed manner. I don't think I ate very much due to being homesick. Sitting at their dining room table with velvet cushions and backs, I waited silently. Mrs. Romo nonstop smiling invited me to partake in the huevos rancheros, cubed fried potatoes, refried beans with home-made tortillas. She asked if I drank coffee. I shook my head yes.

Mr. and Mrs. Romo had two restaurants. One in Kenosha which is south of Racine and one in Burlington west of Racine. Messala and I spent a lot of time helping out in the restaurant in Burlington. It was an old A&W drive-in. The Romos continued serving the same menu items, but it wasn't franchised anymore; it was theirs. I got my work ethic start at that drive-in. It would pay off in my future when I would get a job working for the City of San Antonio after I was discharged from the US Army.

I learned a lot from the Romos. I spent most of my time with Mrs. Romo. She taught me how to run the grill and fryers. She even taught me to make the root beer. I don't think I remember Mrs. Romo ever being angry. It was something that I wasn't accustomed to. My biological mother was always angry. Mrs. Romo was always so gentle and kind to me. She had the softest voice. The voice of an angel.

I had forgotten about all the things I learned about the way G-d wanted me to live. Mrs. Romo was G-d's way of reinforcing that. That lady shone a true example of G-d's love. A true Christian. But I still had not admitted that Jesus Christ died for my sins. Nobody led me in the sinner's prayer. Nobody asked me if I wanted to be baptized. I speak of baptism being submerged in water. Not the Catholic way when an infant has water sprinkled on their head.

I was defiant, full of anger, and rebellious. My lack of nurturing from my mother attributed to it, but as we grow older, we develop our personalities and G-d holds us responsible because we know right from wrong. It's the paths that we choose that will decide our destiny. G-d Almighty gives us free will, and when we use that free will, there are consequences for every decision and action in our lives. I was no different. It wasn't his will for my life to be the way it was. I chose it for myself.

G-d's Holy Spirit brings conviction. I know it now as a man and can distinguish it right away. I recall the first time I think I felt his conviction. I felt so bad that I carried it with me through my life.

One day, Mrs. Romo told me to mow the grass at the drive-in. I remember getting angry at her and telling her, "You must think I'm your slave. I'm always doing everything around here for nothing."

It was the furthest thing from the truth; she would give me money. G-d had removed me from an environment where a woman that didn't love me and place me with a woman who, although I was not her biological son, was willing to treat me as if I was.

Her response was "Okay, Steven, go have a seat by the tree you were just under."

I gladly complied. With a cocky smile on my face as I strolled, thinking I showed her. I just got over. I'll turn the tables and start controlling this. Just as Satan wanted me to act. Ungrateful, arrogant, and full of pride. I went back and sat down and watched her try to start the hand-pull lawn mower. Messala came out immediately and tried to assist her. She asked him to go back in and tend to the customers. He complied and went back inside. The haughty smile I was wearing started to fade.

As the conviction of the Holy Spirit fell on me, I rose to my feet and went over to her and asked her if I could help her start the motor. She said gently in her soft voice, "No, Steven, go back to your tree."

I said, "Please, Mrs. Romo. If my dad saw me letting you do this while I was sitting under a tree, he would be ashamed of me."

G-d was seeing me and he was not happy with me. I think not only would my dad would be ashamed of me but also my Heavenly Father that sent me the conviction. In the absence of my dad, I was ashamed of myself at that very moment. Again, she calmly said, "Steven, go back to your tree."

I turned and hung my head in shame and walked off. I truly was ashamed of myself. She eventually started the mower and cut the grass herself.

I learned a valuable lesson that day. Here I was treated so well by Mrs. Romo all the time and I returned her good with evil. Mrs. Romo followed the teaching of our Lord and the Holy Scriptures.

1 Peter 3:9 says, "Do not repay evil with evil or insult with insult, but with blessing, because to this you were called so that you may inherit a blessing."

I was so ashamed of myself. Nothing I said could change her mind.

The weekends at the Romos' home were rest and relaxation. The Romos had a son, Ramiro Junior. He was thin but fit. He usually was in a golfing style shirt, casual style shorts, and sandals. Like the Romos, he was a very kind individual. He would stop by to see his mother and father. They would drink coffee and visit. I guess they were catching up on things as most families would do. I'm guessing because I didn't know what normal families did. The Romos had a small grandson, about two or three years old. His name was Tony. You guessed it, he was the Tony Romo, the star quarter back of the Dallas Cowboys. At the time, I wouldn't have never known I was standing next to a pro NFL quarterback. Then again, Tony, his parents, and his grandparents, the Romos, didn't know it either.

My dad must have worked some magic or something because he had arranged with the court to have me return to Racine where I could legally live with him and my stepmother Annette. The day he picked me up, I was so happy to leave. Even though the Romos treated me so well, I wanted to get back home to the environment I was accustomed to. The Romos and I said our goodbyes. Mrs. Romo told me to behave because G-d was always watching what I do. With everyone smiling, I embraced Mrs. Romo with a big hug. It felt good. It was real. She really did care about me as a son. My dad and I left and started our way back home to Racine.

I must have been sixteen years old. It wasn't long and I picked up where I had left off. I was about to move up to the next level in what Satan had wanted me to do. After all I had learned, I left Jesus back at the Romos. I didn't have time for Jesus. I had not accepted him as my Lord and personal savior yet. But I had been exposed to him and the scriptures. I had more important things to do the devil would whisper to me. I started drinking beer and smoking marijuana. I didn't smoke it very often. I didn't like the feeling it gave me. Most of the time I smoked it, I did it to try to be cool and show everyone I was not a nerd. Nerd was an expression used back then. The sitcom *Happy Days* made it a popular word to use. I didn't want to be labeled a nerd. Instead, I would go with the flow of the world.

Matthew 7:13 says, "Enter through the narrow gate. For wide is the gate and broad is the road that leads to destruction, and many enter through it."

Back before being court ordered to live with the Romo's, I had only petty stole. As I grew older, every year, I got braver and braver. Burglarizing houses, going with friends that had cars, and stealing things from patios at night. After, selling the goods for spending money.

One time, walking with my friend Robert through Humble Park, we noticed two couples who appeared to be intoxicated. We walked past them as they giggled and played on the swings together. It was really late, maybe 1:00 a.m. As we walked, I thought they would be an easy target. I asked Robert if he wanted to rob them. Without hesitation and with a sinister smile, he agreed. We reached for bandanas we had in our back pockets. We folded them like a cowboys and put it over our faces like when they'd rob a stagecoach. We returned to them with large lockblade knives opened and demanded all their money. The young girls began crying and the two guys seemed intimidated by the reflection of the street light that flashed on our blade. I gave instruction for them to all hurry up. They quickly complied, throwing money and valuables close together about ten feet in front of them. With my eyes fixed on them, Robert and I collected the cash and what jewelry they relinquished.

Both me and Robert bolted across Twenty-First street with our destination being the train track. Once we reached them, we'd just walk west. We were safely away.

There were houses on the south side of the tracks, but as the track began to elevate, the houses got lower and lower down steep embankments. As the Lathrop Street viaduct came into view, we really knew we made it. After we crossed the viaduct, we'd be in our own neighborhood again. We knew all the streets and yards to make an escape had the authorities rolled up on us unexpectedly.

We were on Republic Avenue; like I said, we knew all the yards. We eluded the police too many times to count in our neighborhood. From gates between garages to boards on privacy fences, I personally installed hinges to make escape a breeze. Eventually, we'd make it to my yard, go in the back door and down the stairs to my second bedroom that was vacated by my brother who had joined the navy.

My dad would call out, "Steven, is that you?"

"Yeah, Dad, it's me."

He'd call out, "Are you staying in?"

"I don't know, yeah, I guess. Can Robert stay over? His mom knows."

He'd always say yes.

Like Malcome Mcdowell in the movie *A Clockwork Orange*, Robert and I began to divide the spoils of our recent heist.

Now Robert had been my best friend for a long time; we liked to do lots of the same things. One thing we enjoyed together was hitting cars with rocks and outrunning the drivers that were angry enough to jump out of their car and give a foot chase after us.

Robert came from a good family. His dad was a hardworking man. His mother worked in some kind of health care. He had eight siblings. Five brothers and three sisters. I always thought all his sisters were pretty. Two were arrogant and one was very sweet. His middle sister was always nice to me. I got along with all his brothers. It was his mother that hated me. You see, she had this notion that her children never did anything wrong. She believed that they were led astray by others. Like she thought I was a bad influence on Robert. She considered me the devil incarnate. She would tell me she didn't want Robert around me as he stood behind her laughing silently, letting me take the fall for repugnant things we enjoyed doing.

We never listened to her. One time, she came knocking on my house door and my dad answered. She told him that I was getting Robert in trouble all the time. That she didn't want me around him. My dad said, "Wait a minute. Steven is bad, I know that he is. He's my son. Don't come to my house acting like Robert is being persuaded by Steven to do anything. He comes knocking on this door looking for him. In fact, he comes here every day."

I don't recall, but if I remember right, my dad closed the door on her. You see, he loved me so much. He hoped that I would change some day. In that same loving way, G-d always hopes that everyone will change. He wanted to see me succeed in life. Just like my heavenly father desired for me do his will. His love has no end. I know that every day when I was living that life. Every morning when I opened my eyes and filled my lungs with air, G-d gave me another chance to change. Only G-d can change the heart of a man.

Ezekiel 36:26 says, "I will give you a new heart and put a new spirit in you; I will remove from you your heart of stone and give you a heart of flesh."

We'd do most things together. We didn't care what his mom said and my dad was lax.

Well, I was dating my first wife. Robert, his girlfriend Maria, me, and my first later to be wife would bowl, shoot pool, and eat out often. We kind of laid off all the monkey business and were spending time with our girlfriends but being careful not to deny our company to each other. Taking late-night cruises, drinking beer with other guys who had cars. We made sure to do this once or twice a week and hang with the girlfriends on weekends.

Chapter 5

December 19, 1983, I was seventeen years old when my Lord blessed me with Kristina. My first little girl. She was such a tiny baby. I loved her so much. She was the best thing that ever happened to me. Surely, this little girl would grow. As she grew, I just knew I'd be loved by her. She'd never stop loving her daddy. She was a skinny little girl.

She had big brown eyes and long black hair. Always smiling, always happy playing. She was the world to me. She was the world to my dad. He loved that little girl. Out of all the bad things I had done in my young life, something finally was good. We were a couple of proud guys, my dad and I. Kristina was my dad's first grandchild. She was the apple of my dad's eye. He spoiled her like the way only a grandpa could do. My stepmom Annette was so very sweet to Kristina also.

I was immature and carefree, thinking about everything in life but the things that mattered. Things like supporting my daughter and her mother. All I did was hang out with my friends a lot and shooting basketball at a church or school yards on different sides of town. Drinking beer and smoking cigarettes. Yeah, I was a real class act. I had my priorities straight (sarcasm). I should have been saving the little money I had instead of spending it on good times with my friends.

I worked odd and end jobs, nothing very long. It wasn't enough to support little Kristina and her mother. My dad supported them mostly.

One day, my dad and I were drinking coffee at the Blue Diamond on Durand Avenue. He said, "Steven, have you ever considered joining the service like my brother?" My dad then said, "My brother was in the army his whole life. Join the service and leave this place, son. The police and the judges know you. If you join the service, they'll forget about your past."

Initially, I said I didn't know. We talked and talked about it lots of times. We talked about to the point where he convinced me to take the ASVAB test (Armed Services Vocational Aptitude Battery). I didn't score high enough to join without a high school diploma. I had dropped out of school in my junior year. To me, school was a waste of time. I had better things to do like hanging out. I would stay hanging out with the wrong crowd, wasting more of my life day by day. Who was I trying to kid? I was the wrong crowd. Still up to no good, causing any kind of havoc was euphoric for me. Fueled by Satan, I continued doing just like he wanted me to do.

Eventually, I started to want to be in the US Army so bad that I decided to enroll in Gateway Technical Institute to get my high school diploma so I could join the army. There was no chance of joining without it. You see, the days were long gone of the judge saying join the service or go to jail. No sir, the military could be selective. As technology advanced and the world was changing. You now had to do things their way or you wouldn't get in.

Microwave ovens were out. Rotary phones were gone to be replaced by push button dialing. VCRs were big. And Atari 2600 was the video game system that had replaced the two lines and a square thing they called pong or TV tennis.

I could go to basic training and (AIT) Advanced Individual training with no problem. The catch was that the only thing that Uncle Sam would offer me was Army Reserves.

Now I had something I was after and that was joining the regular army. I knew I had to obtain this diploma or I'd never be able to enlist. If it wasn't for the criteria of the US Army, I probably would have abandoned this endeavor also. So I worked and I worked until the day I was finally awarded my adult high school diploma. It was my ticket to the army.

My recruiter did all my paperwork. He took me to eat on his dime. He would visit with me at his office downtown. This was a ploy to ensure I would truly enlist. Kind of buttering you up like a piece of bread. I fell for it. Hook, line, and sinker.

I took my oath of enlistment in February 1985. It was in Milwaukee, Wisconsin. Man, did they treat me and the other guys joining like kings. A nice hotel room and fine food.

Some guy in a military uniform that I vaguely remember. I couldn't tell you if he was wearing an army, navy, air force, or a marine uniform. My mind was wandering as he gave the instruction of what we were all about to do. He asked if there were any questions. All of us guys in the room glanced at each other, making nanosecond eye contact with each other. Nobody had a question, so he proceeded. He instructed everyone to raise their right hand and repeat after him.

"I, Steven Salas, do solemnly swear that I will support and defend the Constitution of the United States against all enemies, foreign and domestic; that I will bear true faith and allegiance to the same; and that I will obey the orders of the President of the United States and the orders of the officers appointed over me, according to regulations and the Uniform Code of Military Justice. So help me G-d."

Back then, we didn't affirm. People loved G-d. Our president loved G-d he wasn't afraid to make that known to our nation. I had the honor of serving under President Ronald Reagan and briefly under President George H. W. Bush. Both Presidents I can say I was very proud to have them as my commanders in chiefs. It wasn't until President Donald Trump took office that you would hear G-d being mentioned by a president without fear of being ridiculed.

It was done. I'm in. I smiled to myself. I finally did something that I could be proud of. I was going to be a soldier. An hour or two before we would depart to General William (Billy) Mitchell International Airport, we had all taken our oaths.

We departed the MEPS station. (Military Entrance Processing Station) out on to the bright Milwaukee Street. A gust of bitter cold wind that came off Lake Michigan chilled me down my back. We were going who knows how far before the bitter cold wind would die down. I was relieved when I saw our sixteen-passenger US government van waiting on us.

Horsing around and laughing, we finally formed a line to board it. With that same military person the led us through our oaths said, "All right now, settle down and listen up, people. Listen up, you people."

That was a phrase I would grow accustomed to for a long time. If everyone had their envelopes with their paperwork. He then ordered everyone to raise their hand with their envelope in it. We all complied as instructed as his eyes scanned down all extended hands. Making sure everyone was holding an envelope. With that being done, he instructed all of us to board the van.

Sooner than expected, we arrived at the airport and were in the terminal. We all filed into a line and boarded the plane. Finding my assigned seat, I buckled up my seat belt and waited for departure. I thought about Kristina; I missed my little girl. Thinking about her made me smile secretly to myself. I gazed out the window at the tarmac. Small scooter type cars with trailers. They looked like small trains. They were whizzing back and forth to the planes to load luggage. Men with short florescent orange-lighted batons gave visual instructions to planes approaching the accordion-like entrance that connected the plane to the terminal. I heard what sounded like a clunk as my plane began to free-wheel back some. As the high pitch of the jet engines increased louder, we finally began to move in reverse. I was on my way to Louisville, Kentucky.

My jet made a couple of turns then stopped as the jet engine winded down as the pilot waited for his clearance for takeoff from the control tower. The jet engines increased their high-pitched unmistakable wine as we moved forward. Rapidly gaining more speed every second and finally lifting off the ground. Like a carnival ride when it first starts. The plane swayed momentarily, tipping side to side briefly then straightening out.

I looked out my window, watching the fluffy clouds. They seemed to have no end to their form. Now and then, another jet would go soaring past in the opposite direction taking businessmen back to their home offices. Family back to loved one. Families waiting to greet them with open arms, thanking G-d for their safe return.

My plane touched down in Louisville. This time, a Specialist E-4 was waiting on our arrival. He held a clipboard and said, "Now you people listen up. I'm going to call off your name when you hear it, say loud and clear, 'Here.'"

Everyone was present and accounted for.

Rudely, he instructed us to follow him. I boarded the OD green (olive drab) school bus. He put the standard transmission into first gear, grinding it a few times then finally finding first. Letting out the clutch, my head jerked back a couple of times before becoming still again.

Driving the forty-mile stretch from Louisville to Fort Knox, I sat back quietly talking to the guy in the seat next to me. As I approached my destination, I could see a sign; the read welcome to Fort Knox Kentucky United States Army Training Center, Home of the 1st Armor Division. I saw some clean-shaved, very fit, very tall men wearing what looked like Smokey the Bear's hats, impeccable starched uniforms with jump boots that shone like mirrors. I could see reflections of objects in their boots as the bus came to a halt in front of them.

This chill ran down my back. A chill of when I looked at the men. I wanted to be like them. I wanted to be a solider.

Dazed and daydreaming, I came back to my senses as the sound of the school bus door folding open. That same sound it made on school field trips. Within seconds of it opening, a drill sergeant boarded the bus and was at the top of the bus stairs back to the windshield hat slightly tipped forward, and with a loud stern voice, he emitted these words, "You people, listen up. When you left home, you were under your parents' care, you are now under my care. You will no longer eat, drink, sleep, walk, talk, or scratch you a—— until someone tells you to do so. I'm going to give you approximately ten seconds to get off this bus and G-d help you if you are the last man off this bus because you better give your soul to G-d because your a—— is mine. Do you understand?"

In which at that moment instinctively, every passenger replied, "Yes, sir."

The drill sergeant yelled, "I can't hear you."

Again came everyone's simultaneous answer, "Yes, sir."

"I still can't hear you. You all sound like a bunch of old ladies."

This time everyone yelling as loud as they could at the same time, "Yes, sir."

About a three-second pause came before he roared at us, "Move, move, move, move your f——king a——s."

Every man on that bus tried to beat the other to the door, creating chaos and what was like a log jam on a river. This almost prevented the others from exiting.

Everyone did their best and finally got off, only to be met by other waiting drill sergeants screaming every vulgarities you could think of. I was used to that. My mom had talked to me that way my whole life. I found my place among the other in the formation. I looked in terror as guys were crying in the front leaning rest position (push-up position); a drill sergeant with one hand on each of his knees halfway squatting down looking into the crying man's eyes and screaming, "Quit your sniveling, you candy a—— fairy, get on your f——king feet."

Having mercy on him only because he was collapsing from muscle failure. His arms could no longer support his own body weight.

Before I could turn straight, a drill sergeant said, "What the f——k are you looking at, Private?"

I mumbled something and he said, "Shut your mouth. I'm asking the questions here, boy."

Before I could respond to his question, he said, "Get on your face and push."

With that, I instantly assumed the front leaning rest position. He screamed again, "I said fu——ing push."

I said, Huh? I don't understand."

He said, "Start doing pushups, you f——king idiot."

So I did. I didn't cry. Years of being called every name in the book by my mother had made me immune to the worst of insults. Within what seemed like seconds, he said, "Recover."

He was using words I never heard before. I was confused because I didn't understand. So I kept pissing him off more.

"Get on your feet, you moron."

With his head looking down at me, I tried to lean backward without losing my balance as he pressed the brim of that Smokey the Bear hat against my forehead. He said, "You better square yourself away or next time, I'm going to knock the living s——it right out of you. Do you understand me?"

I replied, "Yes, sir."

He shouted back, "Don't call me, sir, I work for a fu——ing living. Say yes, Drill Sergeant."

I said, "Yes, Drill Sergeant."

He yelled, "Sound off like you have a set."

As loud as I could, I said, "Yes, Drill Sergeant."

Sternly, he said, "Thank you very much. Now get at f——king attention and don't move until you are instructed to."

I complied and again replied, "Yes, Drill Sergeant."

I had just met Drill Sergeant Friedman.

The next eight weeks were grueling. We marched everywhere we went. Toting an M16-A1 rifle and a full pack of army equipment started to physically strengthen my body. I used muscles I never knew I had. I learned a high standard discipline, respect for others and respect for myself. I kind of felt like I fit in. It kind of felt like a family to me. Heck, it was a family. Drill Sergeant Freidman said he was my mother, father, brother, sister, aunt, and uncle. All soldiers were my brothers. He said there was no room for individualism in his army. He said, "There's no I in the word army." My barracks, my chow hall, my sidewalk, my lawn. Everything was his. And you'd better not dare disrespect anything that was his (technically, US Army property). I did my best to pay attention and learn all that was being taught to me in this strange new way.

A person can take only so much. If you are training to be a soldier, it takes time to fully discipline yourself totally. One day, Drill Sergeant Freidman got in my face as he normally did and said, "Eye to the front, hands closed and arms slightly bent running along the seams of your pant. Straighten your back, don't slouch. You got that numb nuts?"

I replied with the words that were every so common. "Yes, Drill Sergeant," only I said it rolling my eyes. Dear G-d in heaven did he come unglued.

He jetted back in front of me and said, "That's a mother——king revoking gesture. I'll have you up on charges, you f——king scumbag. I will have you prosecuted under the UCMJ (Uniform Code of Military Justice). You'll spend the rest of your enlistment in Fort Leavenworth. Don't you ever roll your eyes and disrespect me again like that or I will tear your fu——ing head off your shoulders, you no good vomit."

Fort Leavenworth was the US Army military prison located in the state of Kansas. I tried to apologize. I said, "I'm sorry, Drill Sergeant," in which I thought the veins in his forehead that were now protruding were about to burst. Then he turned it down a couple of notches and said something I'll remember as long as I live.

He said, "Salas, don't you ever use the word sorry in my army. In my army, the word sorry is used for only one reason. That when I have to call up your mama and say ma'am, I'm sorry your son was killed today." He turned with precision, making a right face, walking off leaving me standing at attention.

I thought as I was standing there, *If he called my mother, she wouldn't care.* The only thing she cared about is if she had to pay to ship me home. That and if the SGLI (Service Member Group Life Insurance) that they gave every enlisted man, stating her as the beneficiary. They'd be better off calling my dad. He's the only one that ever cared about me.

Now one day we had formation, Drill Sergeant Freidman asked if anyone wanted to attend a church service right off base. After church service, they want to serve you homemade food and soft drinks. Regular Sunday service, we were only granted to worship for one hour and then you had to be back at the barracks. It was a Sunday and a few hours away from the wooden floor, my World War II barracks at Bravo Company 19th battalion 4th Training Brigade was a treat. Most of us men accepted the offer. We loaded onto a government bus and made our way to somewhere I couldn't tell you. I looked at all the trees, properties, as we rode to our destination.

We arrived at this small country church in the middle of nowhere and we were warmly greeted by its parishioners. Men and women dressed in their Sunday best. Each shaking our hands as we entered the sanctuary. We filed into the pews. Now this was a church like I never had been to before. The preacher preached his sermon walking back and forth across the altar. Reading the words of G-d from the Holy Scriptures. He was reading, then he'd look up and then back down again. I remember when he got to these word, something started to happen to me. John 14:6 says, "Jesus answered, 'I am the way and the truth and the life. No one comes to the Father except through me. He said are you tired of the way you are living? Come to Jesus.'" John 6:37 says, "All that the Father giveth me shall come to me; and him that cometh to me I will in no wise cast out." Most of my life, I felt like an outcast. But G-d said, "I won't cast you out."

This feeling that I never felt before was getting stronger and stronger. Suddenly, there was a man from this church next to me. He said, "Son, don't you fight it. That's Holy Ghost. Give it to Jesus, son, give it to Jesus."

The preacher raised his voice. He wasn't yelling. It was to make sure everyone heard what he was saying. Matthew 11:28–30 says, "Come to me, all you who are weary and burdened, and I will give you rest. Take my yoke upon you and learn from me, for I am gentle and humble in heart, and you will find rest for your souls. For my yoke is easy and my burden is light." All that I had ever done in my life started to come back to my memory. From stealing penny candy to robbing those two young couples in the park. Suddenly, it was all that I could take. I couldn't suppress it any longer. I literally collapsed on this man. My legs buckled and I could barely stand. He grabbed me and stood me up while hugging me. The kind of hug where you know they care. He consoled me as I began to cry so hard. I cried like a little baby. The man said, "Give it to Jesus, son. Let him have it all. He wants to take it all from you. Let it all out, son, you don't have to carry it with you no more."

Elohim, The Spirit of the Great I am was upon me. The same G-d who had spoke to Moses on Mount Sinai. The Same G-d who called out Adam asking him, "Who told you that you were naked?" The same G-d who asked Cain, "Where is your brother, Cain? What have you done? Listen. Your brother's blood cries out to me from the ground." That same G-d who was the manifestation of Jesus Christ in the flesh.

Nineteen short years of pain, ridicule, and rejection. My filthy sin and all that I had ever done in my short life, G-d's Spirit was removing them. I had just had a Holy Ghost experience. After I finally stopped crying, I felt so refreshed. I felt so much better. The man asked me, "Do you want to go up to the altar and receive Jesus as your Lord and Savior?"

I said, "I don't know how to."

He said, "I'm going with you, son."

I agreed and we exited the pew I was in and made my way with him to the altar. The preacher was there still giving me and all others who wanted to receive Jesus time to reach the church's altar. Other soldiers were being escorted by other men of the church. Some were still sobbing. As we knelt down before G-d in the presence of man. I heard the word of the Holy Scriptures being preached from the preacher of this church. Matthew 10:32 says, "Who ever acknowledges me before others I will acknowledge them before my father."

The preacher said, "You have made the most important decision of your life. I'm going to lead you in the sinner's prayer. You are freely receiving Jesus Christ as your Lord and Savior today, men. Repeat after me, men."

I repeated these words, "Dear G-d in heaven, I come to you in the name of Jesus. I acknowledge to You that I am a sinner, and I am sorry for my sins and the life that I have lived. I need your forgiveness. I believe that your only begotten Son Jesus Christ shed His precious blood on the cross at Calvary and died for my sins, and I am now willing to turn from my sin. You said in Your Holy Word, Romans 10:9, that if I confess the Lord our G-d and believe in our hearts that G-d raised Jesus from the dead, I shall be saved.

"Right now, I confess Jesus as the Lord of my soul. With my heart, I believe that G-d raised Jesus from the dead. This very moment I accept Jesus Christ as my own personal Savior and according to His Word, right now, I am saved. Thank you, Jesus, for your unlimited grace which has saved me from my sins. I thank you, Jesus, that your grace has allowed to lead me to repentance. Therefore, Lord Jesus, transform my life so that I may bring glory and honor to you alone and not to myself.

"Thank you, Jesus, for dying for me and giving me eternal life. Amen."

The preacher said, "Thank you, Jesus. Men, what you just did is the best thing you could ever do in your life. Wherever you get stationed following your training. Get yourself a Bible and study G-d's word. Meditate on his word. Get into a Bible-believing church, pray, and fellowship with other believers."

Following that, we all started to partake in the delicious food the ladies of this church had made for us. I hadn't tasted food like this in a while. Chow hall food is what we ate every day. There's something about when a woman cooks something compared to an army cook. When we finished with our meals, we loaded back aboard the bus that brought us and headed back to Fort Knox back to basic training.

After my eight weeks were completed, my basic training was over It was now time for me to headed to Fort Leonardwood, Missouri. After eight weeks of heavy equipment operator school, I was officially United States GI.

Chapter 6

I arrived in Fort Leonardwood, Missouri, to start my training as a 62J general construction equipment operator. It was either March or April. I had eight weeks of more training to complete and I was eager to begin.

My time went by very fast. I seemed to be good at what I was doing. The heavy machinery interested me very much. So I was eager to learn all that I could. At the same time, it was fun. I heard it said that if you enjoy your job, you'll never work a day in your life. That may be so, but does that include properly wearing a uniform? Highly shining your boots nightly, keeping shaved and groomed to standards? This was the United States Army.

I completed my MOS and waiting now for orders to be cut for me. I was also promoted to Private First Class.

My orders arrived. Lots of GIs were gone, having received their orders already. There were only a few of us left in the barracks. They were really empty. We weren't having to make formal formations because the rest of us were waiting on order for a duty assignment. One day, the CQ (Charge of Quarters) yelled for me. "Salas," I heard my name being shouted. I immediately flew off my bunk and headed for his desk in the hallway.

I came to parade rest in front of him, saying, "Private First Class Salas reporting as ordered, Sergeant."

He said, "Knock that off. Here we're laidback. Do you like sauerkraut, Salas?"

I said, "Say it again, Sergeant."

He said, "Do you like bratwurst and sauerkraut? You got orders for Germany." He handed them to me and said, "You can go."

As I walked away reading them, he said, "Salas."

I said, "Yes, Sergeant."

"Are any of you getting pizza tonight?"

I said, "Yes, Sergeant."

He said, "Do me a favor and throw a couple of slices my way."

I said, "Yes, Sergeant."

Later that evening when rates were lower, I got a couple of rolls of quarters and headed to the phone booth to call my dad. I dialed his number, pushing each number carefully, making sure not to mis-dial. I didn't want to waste any of my quarters. The phone began to ring. After a few times, my dad picked up and said hello. I said, "Dad," and he answered, "Yes, mi hijo."

"Hey, how are you?"

"I'm good and you."

"I'm good. Tell my wife to get on the other line."

I asked how Krissy (Kristina) was doing? My dad said that him and Krissy were eating Graham crackers and milk before I called. My wife picked up and said, "Hey, Steven."

I said, "Well, I got orders today for Germany."

My dad replied, "Germany, wow, I don't know if my brother ever went there."

My dad's brother was a career soldier. He was out now and living in San Antonio, Texas.

I said, "Yep, Germany. I get a week's leave and then I have to report there. I'll be home soon and we'll talk more."

We all said our goodbyes and we hung up. The pay phone ate up most of the roll of quarters. It returned a few. There were enough to shoot a game of pool or two.

A few days later, I was on a plane to O'Hara International in Chicago, Illinois. My plane landed and I walked off the plane greeted by my dad, wife, and Krissy. It was a good feeling to be close to home. Chicago to Racine is a forty-five-minute drive up IH-94 going north. My time on leave seemed to go so fast. Back home, I met up with some of my old friends. By then, everyone knew that the troublemaker of the neighborhood was different. I had a completely different attitude thanks to Uncle Sam. After I had finished my leave, my dad, wife, and Krissy took me back to the airport so I could catch my flight to Frankfurt, Germany. The speaker announced my flight departure and I had to board. I hugged my wife and daughter.

My dad and I approached each other face-to-face. I said, "Well, I got to be going, Dad."

My dad extended his hand to shake mine as he turned his head completely away from me. I heard him say, "I'll be seeing you, Steven."

This great dad I had that G-d chose to be my dad was turning so I wouldn't see him cry. I let him be. I let his hand go. As he walked toward the hall way of my terminal, I watched him in his jeans, golfing shirt, tennis shoes, and baseball cap as he pretended to be interested in something on the wall. Looking at whatever he was looking at, I saw him reach and wipe his eyes.

My whole life my dad would say, "Don't cry. Don't show weakness. A Salas doesn't cry or show weakness. If you have to cry, go hide somewhere so nobody sees you." My poor Pops, where was he supposed to hide in the busiest airport in the United States? I couldn't help but feel so bad for him. He loved me so much.

Chapter 7

My flight landed at Rhein-Main Air Force Base in the Federal Republic of Germany in November 1986. After being briefed on the some of the laws of the country, I headed out of the Flughafen (German for airport) to another military office to get orders for the base I was to be assigned to. My name was called shortly after. I heard my name called loud. I identified myself by raising my hand and responded with "Here, Sergeant," as I quickly approached his desk then assumed the position of parade rest. The proper stance given when reporting to an NCO (noncommissioned officer) rendering the respect he was entitled to. He said, "You're staying here in Frankfurt." I acknowledged. I took the orders he handed to me and was dismissed.

Within forty-five minutes, I was in a government van flying down the Autobahn. Arriving very quickly to my destination as we approached the gate of Camp Escborne. The first thing I saw was a soldier coming out of the guard shack. Wearing his LBE (low bearing equipment) and carrying a M16-A1 rifle, he approached the van. After checking our IDs, he gestured to the other soldier at the gate to open it so we could proceed. Through the gate down a long road to a building next to what looked like a giant bubble. A bubble more long than round. I fixed my eyes on it as we approached the parking lot of the Battalion Headquarters. Walking to the entrance of the 317th Engineer Battalion 130 Engineer Brigade. My escort reached for the door handle of the building.

Inside the battalion headquarters I was told I was assigned to Delta Company. The Delta Dogs is what we were called. The CQ's assistant, usually an E-4 and below, showed up later to escort me to

48

the Delta Company Barracks. I don't recall who it was that picked me up to show me the way to Delta Company. We walked past the enlisted club that looked dead. There were some JP-4 tanks that came into view as we walked. Suddenly I asked, "Hey, what is that giant bubble thing?"

The soldier answered, "Oh, that's our gym."

I thought, *Gym? That like no gym I've ever seen before.* We got to Delta Company barracks and I was shown to the room I'd be staying in. It resembled a college dorm. The long highly shined waxed floors and the smell of Clorox was an indication that this was no college dorm. It was a multifloor army barracks.

About halfway down the hall, we stopped facing a room on our right side. The CQ's assistant gave a few raps on the door with two of his phalanges of his right hand. From within, a voice said to enter. The CQ's assistant said, "This is Salas, he's your new roommate."

He said this then turned and walked away. The guy standing in front of me was slender, medium built with a thin but full mustache. His hair wasn't bald because we were in permanent party. The term used for not being in recruit training anymore.

The soldier extended his hand with a wide white smile and said, "I'm Richards from Appleton, Wisconsin."

"No kidding? I'm Salas. I'm from Racine, Wisconsin."

Imagine that all the way around the world here in Europe and we're from the same state.

He showed me my bunk and helped me unpack my OD green duffel bag. We talked and got to know each other more. Then he invited me for a beer at the enlisted club on base.

We arrived walking to the enlisted club within minutes The walk was short; it was very close to the barracks. We went inside. It was dark and empty. Nobody was there. It reminded me of a VFW banquet hall. The way the tables and chairs were arranged it look like a wedding reception had just ended with the exception of it being immaculate. We ordered Pilsner, my first German bier. I don't remember what the brand was, us GIs just called them flippy's. We called them that because the bottle didn't have a cap like US beer. They had this hinged cap with a rubber gasket. They were kind of like very old canning jars. Why would you need that kind of cap, I don't know. I guess in case you wanted to save some for latter.

All this time, G-d was the furthest from my mind. I hadn't given him much thought let alone prayer. I was beginning my three-year tour. I was assigned to Headquarters Platoon 4th Squad. Our squad leader was an E-5 buck sergeant. There was Carson, Sachtleben, Nowakowski, Swift, and myself in my squad.

We'd go to the motor pool daily to do maintenance on our equipment in the event the Russians crossed the Fulda Gap. This was an area near the Czech border. Over and over, we'd work and train.

It was the second week of April 1987. I went the motor pool like any other day. Sergeant Johnson and I were walking together. We were going down to load a caterpillar D-7 bulldozer on a low boy trailer. It was going to be used on some mission our section had been assigned to. Sergeant Johnson watched as I loaded the bulldozer on the trailer that was hooked to M-915 tractor trailer truck. This was the army's heavy equipment hauler. It was equipped with sixteen gears and an engine retarder to slow the truck's heavy load down without having to use you air brakes so much.

I finished loading the bulldozer. I dismounted it and started pulling out chains and load binders. I started rigging up the equipment to the low boy. Then I began hooking up the load binders to the chains. While up on the low boy, I started compressing a load binder; within a split second, the chain whipped back as it broke, striking in the front of my head. The only thing I remember Sergeant Johnson saying was "Did it get ya?"

Before I could answer, I fell off the low boy backward, striking my head a second time on the rocks on the ground. The back of my head hit hard as I fell onto the extra large rocks that was throughout our parking area.

The next thing that happened was I regained consciousness. I felt Sergeant Johnson holding a t-shirt, applying direct pressure on my head as the pickup was transporting me as fast as it could to a hospital.

I looked down toward my feet and saw a giant puddle of blood and I began to breathe very hard. As another soldier was undoing my shoe laces, unbuckling my belt and unbuttoning my shirt the way we were all taught to prevent shock. Sergeant Johnson reassured me I was okay. But there was so much blood, I just didn't believe him.

At the hospital, I had a CT Scan/MRI done and stitched my head. They kept me overnight for observation. The next day, I was released as the army doctor said I was okay. So off I went. A few days off work and light duty when I returned. Back to the normal routine. "Hey, it was nothing. You're a soldier," I told myself. I brushed that injury off like it was nothing.

I started getting terrible headaches and bouts of severe dizziness. I went back to the doctors and they said it was normal. I also noticed I became more agitated easily. Sleeping became very difficult. And my memory was vague at times. Mostly short term. Something more was definitely going on and I knew it. Being young, you think you can handle anything that comes your way. So I started to ignore the symptoms.

Chapter 8

F all began in Germany in October. The year was 1987. My wife
was pregnant with our second child. As Halloween approached,
the baby was getting closer to being born. Unfortunately for
Kristina, my oldest daughter, she wouldn't be trick or treating this
year.

Erika Salas was born on October 31, 1987. She was such a precious baby. Kristina was a big sister and I was dad to a newborn
again. It was so great being a dad. Playing with my little girls and
getting them whatever they wanted at the toy store. I always gave my
girls whatever they wanted. As a child, I was always barked at by my
mother. Telling me there wasn't enough money put it back.

So we had fun. They had fun with the toys they wanted and I
had fun making sure they were never disappointed like me.

The girls would play and play. They had dolls they had games
they had Legos, everything you could think of. Even a couple boy
toys. That I persuaded them into getting just so I could play with
them. It was my way of making up what my mother had deprived me
of. We had an AFX slot car racing track. Boy, did I have fun with it.

One evening, I had to pull guard duty. It was always a twenty-
four-hour thing. In between shifts, I would call home to see how
thing were going at my house and how Kristina and Erika were
doing. Sometimes, I'd call late to talk to my wife. She was a stay-at-
home mom so she was able to stay up late.

Well, I called home about 2300 hours (11:00 p.m.) and I got
no answer. I rang the house phone again and again, still no answer. I
had this gut feeling something wasn't right. The sergeant on duty in
charge of the guard duty let me go home after telling him something

52

might be wrong. He said, "Just make sure you're back for you next shift."

I acknowledged his order and left out the gate in my lime-green 1973 VW beetle (Slug Bug). I didn't live far from my post. Arriving home, I raced up the stairs. I put my key in the door and opened it. There were a couple lights on and it was quiet. Kristina and Erika were sound asleep in their beds. Their mother was nowhere to be found. I asked a neighbor to keep an eye on the girls and I started searching the complex for her. Now I don't know where this comes, from but I get these feelings. When things aren't right. The expression of a gut feeling is what I had.

So following this instinct, I knock on this neighbor's door who was an MP. He came to the door acting like he had been awakened by me. Fake yawning I asked, "Where's my wife?"

He said, "She isn't here," while keeping up his charade.

I said, "I know she is."

He invited me in to check for myself. She had already slipped out. I declined his invitation. The same gut feeling instinct told me to go down to the downstairs hall. When I did, I caught her walking back to the apartment. I became angry and asked what she was doing. She lied and said she was walking. What about the girls? Why did you leave them alone so late at night. She started to argue saying she was gone a few minutes. She admitted to her infidelity, saying she only kissed him. I felt like I had been stabbed through the heart. Betrayed by the one who vowed to love me. Did I turn to G-d? No, I had turned away from G-d is why my world was coming apart. It was coming apart, only I didn't realize it at the moment.

I tried to live it down. I was impossible. The thoughts plagued my mind constantly. I couldn't trust her anymore. My headaches, dizziness, and memory problems continued. And my ears started to ring. It would drive me nuts. To the point of having to sleep with the TV every night so it would block it out.

My tour in Germany eventfully came to an end in November of 1989. My wife, the girls, and I went back to the United States.

Chapter 9

I had received orders to Fort Campbell, Home of the 101st
Airborne Division, the Screaming Eagles. My family followed
with me this time. We got temporary housing and help finding
permanent housing in Clarksville, Tennessee. We eventfully rented a
mobile home. Nothing fancy, it suited us just fine. On February 27,
1990, my third daughter, Angel Salas, was born. She was little and
healthy just like her two older sisters. She was my little baby girl. My
spoiled little baby. They say that the youngest is the most spoiled. It's
true, but I didn't love her more than Krissy or Erika. I knew what it's
like to feel less loved. I didn't want any of these precious gifts from
G-d to ever feel that way. If I had one banana, I broke it into three
equal shares for each of them. At the store, they picked out their own
toys. There was no favoritism. The same way our heavenly father
is with all of us. He lets his sun shine on good and the bad. That's
what Mrs. Romo used to tell me. G-d loves us all the same. He wants
everyone to have eternal life. He wants everyone to receive salvation
through his son Jesus Christ. His offer is to all not just a selected few.

2 Peter 3:9 says, "The Lord is not slow in keeping his promise,
as some understand slowness. Instead he is patient with you, not
wanting anyone to perish, but everyone to come to repentance."

At work in formation, I was asked to go to the Air Assault
School which I happily accepted. The course is a grueling ten days
of physical training combined with classroom curriculum. It consists
of rapelling, rigging, and sling-loading all from helicopters. Upon
completion if you were able to endure and finish, you were given the
honor of wearing the 101st Airborne Division's Air Assault wings. It
was a silver badge worn on the chest. The badge had a front view of

a UH-1 Huey with wings on each side of the helicopter. I graduated Air Assault School on April 30, 1990, as Roster # 11 Class 28-90

My headaches, dizzy spells, ear ringing, and agitation were still bothering me from my TBI. I would go to the army doctor, but they'd say nothing was wrong. I'd get angry because I knew there was. Even worse, I knew there was and nobody would help me.

In May of 1990, I was honorably discharged from the US Army. It felt strange not doing my regular army routine every day. I didn't have to shine my boots anymore and I deliberately left my entire face unshaved. I didn't know what that felt like in five years. I packed my family up and headed home. It would be so good to see my dad again.

Arriving home and getting settled in was my next challenge. I would have to find good enough work to support my family. With my experience driving a semi truck and knowing how to operate heavy equipment and help from G-d, I knew I would succeed. I landed a job with a sewer and water contractor. I only worked there for about six months. Like I said, I was easily agitated. I got into an argument with the owner's son. Like anyone would know, I lost the argument and was terminated. I started thinking I never liked Racine. I never did any good here. Why am I still living here?

Chapter 10

After that brief stay at my dad's, I had saved enough money to move to San Antonio. I arrived there on Christmas Day 1990. We stayed at a motel on Fisher Road next to a Diamond Shamrock gas station on IH35 south right before the town of Lytle.

My wife and I both had family here. I dropped my wife at her sisters with my three girls, then started driving around San Antonio. I cruised the empty streets, looking for a place to eat. There wasn't a soul around. Like an episode from the 1960's series *The Twilight Zone*. It was like I was the only person in the whole town. Not really, everyone was in their homes with family. Sharing tamales, turkey, ham, and other delicious food. Joy and laughter in the packed Southside houses of the Mexican working middle class.

Turning off Military Drive and heading briefly south on Pleasanton Road, a neon sign came into sight. Yes, I thought, it's open. I pulled into the parking lot of Griff's Hamburgers to eat my first meal in San Antonio, Texas.

I walked to the counter at the same time a petite Spanish woman approached me to take my order. I say Spanish because of her European features. She looked Anglo and had the most striking green eyes I had ever seen. Being of Spanish descent myself, I knocked it off right away. I had red hair, fair skin, and freckles. I had the MC1R gene (the recessive gene that gives people red hair) and there was no disputing it.

I got a cheese burger, fries, and Coke. I found a completely empty dining area. It was as empty as the San Antonio streets. I ate my meal while scanning the *San Antonio Light* newspaper (a newspaper now out of business). I circled potential jobs running construction equipment.

Rubbing my right eye trying desperately to relieve the sharp intense pain that was accompanied by my whole right side of my head hurting. My ears were ringing and I felt sick to my stomach. I couldn't eat anymore. I had experienced this so many times before.

I abandoned my meal and went to my car. I knew what to do. The only thing that seemed to help was to close my eyes and relax in silence.

Right after the first of the year, I found work at Bexar Electric (pronounced Bear). Bexar is the county name of the City of San Antonio. I heard or read that Bexar was the name of an Indian Chief back before San Antonio became really established. The story goes this Chief's name was Bear. He was illiterate. And when he was asked to sign his name where it was printed on some documents, he drew an X. Thus the name of the county becoming Bexar instead of Bear.

So I was hired at Bexar Electric as a backhoe operator. I was disciplined well and never missed work. I had a responsibility of a wife and three daughters. The girls were growing and it seemed like they always needed shoes. Their feet grew like weeds.

Some places, people are just different. Bexar Electric seemed like they had a lot of little clicks in the company. If you weren't part of the click, you weren't accepted. Well, I wasn't part of a click. My agitation problem from my TBI had me on edge a lot. There wasn't a whole lot I would take verbally without firing back. Whenever I had a difference with someone, I'd spew my venom, a mixture of words of profanity, usually making them back off of me. I would think after the dispute ended. Who is that idiot to yell at me? I've been yelled at all my life. What I endured verbally in the army was acceptable. The person had earned the uniform and the rank. These civilians (a widely used expression to describe someone not in or never a member of the armed forces) as I looked at them they haven't earned either one. Rank or a uniform. So they were not above me. These arguments happened many times over.

I came in one morning and my boss, Mr. Starling, said, "Steve, we know you're not happy here and we're not happy with you. I'm going to have to let you go."

"Fine, I'm out of this joint," I said. I left and went home to my apartment on West Avenue, north of IH-10.

Day after day, I applied at different places. I was between jobs. So that's all I did. One day, while cruising down West Avenue and finishing up my job search for the day, I turned onto Basse Road. I noticed these two Harley Davidson motorcycles chained to a tree with a For Sale sign in front of them. I pulled into the large gravel driveway of the residence so I could take a closer look at them. I was startled as the owner of the residence emerged from the front door.

I was taken back for a moment, telling him I was just looking at them. His name was Dan Chandler and he would become my very first friend in San Antonio. Dan approached me. He had shoulder-length hair and a long pointed goatee. He had on KD sunglasses that I'm sure he got from Bryce's Cycles on West Avenue down the street. He was wearing an oversized t-shirt with Bugs Bunny and Daffy Duck on it, and it was covered in grease like he had been using it as a shop rag or had been rolling around in grease. His faded jeans were a size too big and he had on cheap white Velcro tennis shoes.

I said, "I like this blue one."

Dan replied, "That one. It's a piece of junk, don't buy it."

My eyes widened in shock. This guy is trying to sell these Harleys, then tells me one is junk. Well, you just killed a potential sale, I thought. Dan told me he worked on both of them. He said that he was selling them for the owners.

Dan said, "Man, it's hot as hell out here, do you want a Dr. Pepper?"

I said, "Sure, thank you."

I didn't have any friends. He gestured his hand in a motion for me to follow him inside. I complied as if he was one of my former superiors in the army. He gave me a soda water as he called them and popped the top on his. He took a great big guzzle, almost finishing half the can. He pulled out a Marlboro Red from a half-spent pack.

He lit it and threw the pack and the lighter on the table at the same time.

He said, "What's your name?"

I said, "Steve, Steve Salas, sir."

Laughing and coughing out a big cloud of smoke at the same time and making me cough uncontrollably, he said, "Sir," laughing again after his smoke-filled lungs were empty. He said, "Just call me Dan."

"All right," I answered.

He asked me basic questions that two strangers ask in an initial conversation. Where do you live, are you married, do you have kids, and where do you work.

I told him all he inquired about me and he told me about his life. I told him I was recently fired from Bexar Electric.

"No kidding, is that place still open?" he said as he extinguished his finished cigarette and taking a swig of what was left of his soda water.

You see, Dan was a great Harley mechanic. I mean, good. He could tear them down and put them back again like he was assembling a preschooler's wooden puzzle. He didn't get out much. He spent most of his time at home. About 90 percent of his time I would say. This guy had such a genuine big heart. Because he did, many would take advantage of Dan. When the labor bill came due from repairs he made to motorcycles. He'd say pay me whenever but they never would. Most would never come back.

I eventfully bought a 1977 Iron Head Sportster from him. It was candy-apple red and I loved it. By then, I landed a job working for the Big Red soda company driving a semi truck, delivering their products. Dan and I would hang out after I finished work and I'd go by his house on weekends with my wife and kids. Dan just loved kids. His wife Betty and him weren't able to have any, so he'd spoil mine. He had big jars of candy and about five different kinds of sweet cereal. You know, you look at someone and you make assumptions. It's very easy for us as humans to judge others. By grace, we have Jesus. Jesus had said not to be this way with each other. When I first saw Dan, I didn't think less of him. I was sure people must look down on him because of his appearance. The scriptures remind us.

James 2:3 says, "If you show special attention to the man wearing fine clothes and say, "Here's a good seat for you," but say to the poor man, "You stand there" or "Sit on the floor by my feet."

1 Samuel 16:7 says, "But the LORD said to Samuel, "Do not consider his appearance or his height, for I have rejected him. The LORD does not look at the things people look at. People look at the outward appearance, but the LORD looks at the heart."

I was a nobody. A stranger off the street. Yet Dan welcomed me into his home, offered me something to drink and eat, and became my friend. He still is my friend to this day. He's one of the kindest, giving people I know.

With my continued hidden health problems from the TBI, I kept it a secret. I was a man and didn't want to appear to be weak. My agitation continued where I found myself yelling at my little girls. After apologizing always. It was like an uncontrollable force would take over and then be gone the next second. These outbursts ended up causing me to lose my job at Big Red. G-d continued blessing me even though I wasn't following him still. I mean, that is some kind of love.

It was October 1992. G-d blessed me with a great job. I had applications everywhere, and on October 26, 1992, I was hired as an equipment operator with the City of San Antonio, Parks and Recreation department. Benefits, medical, vision, dental insurance, and retirement. I sold the Sportster and moved up to a 1977 Shovelhead Electra Glide. G-d was continually blessing me and I don't know why. I wasn't obedient to him. I worked for the Parks department for around eight months. I had applied for other jobs with the city and I moved to Solid Waste to be a recycle truck driver and got a decent pay increase.

Things seem to be going so good when I found out my wife was having an affair behind my back. She ran off with this guy, leaving me to care for the girls. It was hard getting them to school and getting to work so I wouldn't be late. The hand of G-d was over me. I didn't realize it at the time. I always had a difficult time recognizing G-d's love for me.

I needed more money and called my dad. He scolded me, saying, "Well, look you're running up the phone bill right now."

I said, "I don't know what to do."

"Don't know what to do," he said. "Be a man. Get a second job, quit making kids, and stay off the phone. I'll talk to you later."

We hung up. I sat there rubbing my hands together nervously in a motion as if trying to warm them. Suddenly the phone rang. I thought it might be the kids' mom, saying she was coming back. I was wrong. It was my dad. He said, "Mi hijo, do you know why I said stay off the phone?"

I said, "No, Dad."

He said, "I'd rather you write me. After we hang up, it's over."

With a letter, I pulled it out in the coffee shop and read it. At night before bed, I read it again. I can read it over and over because it doesn't end. He said, "I'm sending you $1,000. Find a second job. That's what a man does."

I said, "Thank you, Dad."

He said, "I'll be seeing you."

I did as I was told. Man, my dad never steered me wrong. He always knew what was best so I listened to him. I loaded my lawn equipment into my truck. I put the girls inside with some dolls and I'd drive around in search of lawns to cut for extra money. G-d always provides. I knocked on a door on Mandalay Street off of San Pedro. Through the window, I could smell the aroma of Tex-Mex cooking. An older woman in her late 60s came to the door wearing a house dress and slippers. She had a big smile, wearing large lenses plastic-framed glasses to see correctly. She said, "Yes, may I help you," with a strong Spanish accent.

I removed my baseball cap from my head and said, "Yes, ma'am. I'm cutting yards to earn extra money and yours looks like it needs it."

She asked, "How much?"

I said, "$15, front and back."

She said, "Front and back, go ahead."

G-d had his hand in everything. I finished, and she paid me and offered me a glass of sweet tea. I eagerly accepted, drinking the entire glass all at once, not stopping for air.

I introduced myself and she introduced herself as Mrs. Alonzo. She was a widow who was caring for her son. He was dying of cirrhosis of the liver. I explained my situation and why I needed work. Mrs. Alonzo was a horse trader (expression deal maker). Today, she was trading. She said, "You cut my grass and I'll drive the girls to school and pick them up."

"Deal." I reached out my hand and we shook.

Philippians 4:19 says, "And my G-d will meet all your needs according to the riches of his glory in Christ Jesus."

This was our routine for weeks. When the grass went dormant, Mrs. Alonzo kept helping me. I guess she felt sorry for me. Maybe she was just being a mother, even though she wasn't my mother. She did what a mother would do. She was an angel that G-d put in my path at the time I needed. It helped me keep my good job at the City of San Antonio.

About three months in the first week of January 1995, I was collecting green plastic recycle bins from the curb for the Solid Waste Department. I moved to that department from the Parks Department.

Standing next to the truck, I would start sorting #1 and #2 plastic, newspaper, metal cans, then brown, clear, and green glass. I'd flip the bin upside down as an indication to the taxpayer and my supervisor that I had been through and collected. As I went for another bin, a city municipal pickup was approaching me. The passenger window lowered as the window regulator hummed. My supervisor Ricardo Salazar said, "Red," as everyone called me because of my red hair and goatee. "You need to come in. Just park the truck, grab the keys, and jump in."

When I got in, I said, "What's up?"

He said, "You have an emergency phone call."

I thought, Oh no, one of my daughters might be hurt. I got back to the crew quarters at North Loop. I picked up the phone. My dad's girlfriend was on the line. She said, "Come home, your dad has passed away."

I dropped the phone and started crying, "No, no, no, no, no, G-d no." I went out of the office and threw a table into some lockers. I heard someone say, "Hey, you better chill out." I fell to my knees and cried uncontrollably. I heard the secretary say, "His father died," as she knelt down holding me, trying to console me.

I went home early and knocked on Mrs. Alonzo's door, trying to hold my tears back telling her my dad passed away. "Aye, mi hijo, I'm so sorry" as she hugged me like a mother hugs a child. She said, "Don't worry go home and rest. I'll bring the girls here, they can stay the night. Now you go rest."

I didn't rest; instead I went and bought a couple of quarts of beer and walked aimlessly like a hobo. I walked through the neighborhood of the Los Angeles Heights area of the city where I lived. After finishing the two quarts of beer, I stopped and bought two more. I walked through the streets, not knowing what to do. After a while, I returned home very intoxicated. Sitting on my couch, I continued drinking. I had a bottle of Jim Beam. I heard something at my kitchen door. It opened and the kids' mother was in the doorway. She extended her arms, saying, "I'm sorry, Steven." Before she could take two steps toward me, I threw the whiskey bottle at her. Missing her, it flew past her head smashing through the kitchen door window. The shattered glass laid on the kitchen floor as I yelled, "Get out of here, you left us."

"I'm going to come back, I was wrong," she said.

I don't remember anything after that moment. I ended up passing out, and when I woke, my Uncle Solomon, his wife Valerie, and my Aunt Sophia were inside my house. They were my mother's half siblings. They had the same father as my mother did. Someone had covered me with a blanket, removed my boots, and put a pillow under my head.

My aunt Sophia was cooking dinner for me. The girls' mother sat silently in a corner chair. I said nothing.

Chapter 11

I had to make arrangements to fly home. It was a difficult task having to plan my dad's funeral. It was too soon for him to die. He was only fifty-seven years old. It wasn't fair. I was mad at G-d. I said so this is what I get. Acting if I was living a Christian life. I wasn't living for G-d. I wanted to lash out at someone. At the funeral, I stood at the entrance door. I didn't want to see my dad lying there. After a while, I looked up and it was my mother standing in front of me. She extended her arms in a gesture to hug me. I started crying and said what? Again I said what? Now you want to hold me. Years ago, my mother told me when your dad dies, she was going to dance with joy. I grinded my teeth in anger and told her, "Well, do your dance. Come on, I want to see you do your dance."

She said, "You're just hurting, Steven. I understand."

I yelled at her, "Understand. You don't understand anything about me. You always told me my dad was no good, but he was good. It was you who was never good. It's you who should be lying there, not my dad. You," I said to her again. She walked off leaving me by myself as I wept.

My dad was cremated like he wanted to be. His ashes were brought back to Texas to where he was born. The town of Millet. It's only a couple of miles south of Dilley. My grandparents are buried there. His ashes were scattered between his mother and father. He was back in Texas. Back home where he belonged

I was real vulnerable because all that I had been through. My kids' mother worked her way back into my life. I guess with the loss of my dad, she figured it would be easy. With my dad passing and all. I let my girls' mother come back and we decided to move to northeast San Antonio. We bought a different house and moved in. I was prospecting for the Christian Brothers MC (prospecting is seeking membership in a motorcycle club).

I was now trying to use G-d to keep my relationship together. Well, your way is not G-d's way when he has different plans. And you can't use G-d for anything. He is the one who decides to use someone for his glory. On a day I don't remember, I got one of those feelings like back in Germany. I drove my city truck home for lunch. As I opened the door, I heard some unusual music playing. It wasn't the type I listened to. I walked down my hall and opened my bedroom door. There she was. The mother of my children getting dressed with the same guy she had been seeing before. She told me, "Steven, I don't know why I do what I do."

By then, there was nothing left. Just an empty void in my heart. I calmly told them both, "Just get out of my house."

She left with him again. This time, I had to file for divorce. My girls came home from school that afternoon. I was home because I went home sick after the incident. I had the vacation so I used it. I sat the girls down and told them, "Girls, your mother left again, and this time, she's not coming back."

All three began to cry. I said, "Don't cry, she'll see you again, she just won't live here. She loves you. She's just confused right now." It gave them no consolation.

When they didn't stop crying, I told them, "Look here, girls, I'll never leave you. If I ever leave you, it will be when a black station wagon will back up in this driveway and zip me up in a plastic bag. They'll carry me out and drive away. Cry then because then for sure I won't be back. Now let's make dinner."

The Christian Brothers didn't seem to care what I was going through and that I was devastated once again. I turned my vest in and got angry with G-d again. Can you believe somehow I wanted to blame G-d for all this? Like Adam blaming G-d. He said, "The woman you put here with me gave me some fruit and I ate it." That's basically what I was saying. Every time she betrayed me, G-d didn't. When she deserted the girls and me, G-d was still there. When she left for good, G-d didn't go.

Deuteronomy 31:6 says, "Be strong and courageous. Do not be afraid or terrified because of them, for the LORD your G-d goes with you; he will never leave you nor forsake you."

So I lived life the best I could. I tried being the best dad I knew how to be. My headaches and dizzy spells were something I just learned to live with. I started having trouble sleeping. My agitation was causing me to lash out at the girls more, only to be filled with terrible guilt later. I started going to bars on my motorcycle and drinking. Drinking would help me sleep better along with having the TV on constantly to stop the ringing in my ears. Traveling from bar to bar and becoming more and more dependent on alcohol. Drinking became a routine of my day. I never was a violent drunk. Lots of people knew who I was. I was a very sociable guy. I inherited this part of my personality from my dad.

One night, I went to a local nearby bar in Kirby, Texas. The name of it was the Pour House. Drinking Lone Star beer and passing time, I recognized some friends I knew. They were with some people I didn't know. A woman introduced as Kate. She was very petite with dark black hair and olive color skin. I'm guessing she was Mediterranean, and her ancestors were from maybe Greece, Italy, Spain, or Portugal. I always made it a habit of studying people. I wanted to know about them completely, who they were, where they were from, and what their story was. I had a story, one most wouldn't believe. I had been through a lot. The conversation was casual and everyone took part in the conversation.

Now don't ever think you can't find Jesus in a bar because you can. He won't be partaking of the things of the world, but you will find his Spirit. G-d is everywhere all the time. He can be where he wants whenever he wants.

Matthew 18:20 says, "For where two or three gather in my name, there am I with them."

In G-ds word, he says he will use the foolishness of the world to shame the wise. Kate and I began to fellowship about our faith. She was amazed at how I had great knowledge of the scriptures. It was the beginning of a friendship. It was a brother/sister type friendship. We'd see each other from time to time, running into each other at motorcycle functions or local bars. She definitely became like a sister to me. The sister I never had. G-d blesses you with things you never have had.

Riding became my passion and I saw different club patches people were wearing. I saw the unity, family structure, and camaraderie these groups shared. Again I had the feeling of wanting to be wanted. The feeling of wanting to belong. The feeling of wanting to be loved. You can never substitute Jesus for anything. Who would be willing to die for you? Who would willfully say you deserve to die, but I'll take your place? So please don't try to make a substitute for Jesus. It seemed like the highway went on forever and the party never ended. I can't understand why G-d would continue to protect and bless me. I wasn't doing my part. The Holy Spirit would convict me. Many great men have disobeyed G-d. I'm not making excuses, but I wasn't the first and I certainly wouldn't be the last. I just don't know why I didn't learn when he would try to steer me back in order. G-d will chastise your life. You cannot be arrogant with him. He says in the scriptures that those who exalt themselves will be humbled. I don't ever think I exalted myself, but I sure wasn't doing what G-d wanted me to be doing.

I've been told when you pray, be specific with G-d. Tell him in detail what you want. So one day, I was sitting on a park bench and I began to pray. I said, "G-d, the next time you send me a wife, I want a good wife, Lord. One that will be faithful to the end and be with me forever." Then that thought came to mind about being specific with G-d about what you want. Go into detail, I was always told. So I said, "One more thing, G-d. I want a petite, beautiful, blonde-haired, blue-eyed with a nice figure. Amen."

My leisure time was spent in the biker scene. I'd hit the biker bars that were local to my side of town. I'd also attend the motorcycle rallies. There was usually one every month. People on motorcycles would gather, drink beer, and socialize. I used to frequent a place called the Back Porch in Greuene, Texas. It was right on the Guadalupe River. It was beautiful relaxing area. Drinking beer, shooting the bull, and occasionally watching the people on inner tubes float by was a every weekend thing. I had a very nice Christian lady named Carol that lived across the street from me that would help me with my youngest daughter Angel. Angel and her daughter attended the same school and liked playing together. Kristina and Erika were now old enough watch themselves for a few hours. I'd always make it home before it was too late.

I guess some time had passed since me and the girls were by ourselves. After a long work week in the hot sun of south Texas, I was ready for a few cold ones and a long ride on my Harley Davidson. Now in the motorcycle world, you have riding clubs, mom and pop clubs, AMA, clubs, support clubs, and outlaw clubs. Each pretty much having less power from the bottom of my list on up. The Bandidos MC (motorcycle club) is the Outlaw 1 percenter (1%ER) club of Texas. The Bandidos controlled everything in the motorcycle world in Texas. They have support clubs that wear the same color patches as they do only they reverse the colors. Bandidos, being red and gold, and the support clubs being gold on red. Colors are a way of telling which club you belong to.

There is no mistaking. You had better be educated on colors if you decided that you want to join the motorcycle scene. You would learn the hard way through intimidation or physical violence if you needed more persuasion.

The Bandidos MC was formed in San Leon, Texas, and some say Houston, Texas, on March 4, 1966. I don't know for sure I was always told Houston. Some might dispute between the two cities. The Bandidos is a subculture secrete society. Its founder was Donald Eugene Chambers, a Vietnam Marine Veteran. He took the red and gold colors of the Marine Corps to use for the club's colors.

In 1972, Don Chambers and another member, Jesse Deal, abducted two drug dealers who they believed cheated them on a drug deal. They took them to the El Paso desert and forced them to dig their own graves. Then shot both in the head and buried them. Subsequently, both men were convicted and given life sentences.

With Chambers in prison, another former Marine, Ronald "Ronnie" Hodge, was elected Nation President of the Bandidos.

In 1983, Chambers was paroled and retired from the club. He settled in El Paso until his death in 1999. He was buried in Houston.

A flat granite grave stone covers his whole plot. It inscribes his name, him being the founder of the club and the quote, "We are the people our parents warned us about."

Now being that I had the discipline from my prior army service, I understood rank structure. I understood that the Bandidos were the highest ranking. I was a trained disciplined soldier so it was easy for me.

Every biker bar and biker rally, the Bandidos were sure to appear at them. Most bikers would show respect to the members by offering their handshake and then by the offer of cold beer which no Bandido ever turned down. There were two ways one could get real close to a Bandido member. One was for them to take a liking to you and the other was to be a Bandido support member. If you were a support club member, you could sit and drink with them all night long.

His first name wasn't known by many. If you did, you better not call him by it. His road name (nickname) was Chuck. He was probably the most well-known Bandido in San Antonio. Everyone who rode a motorcycle knew him. He never bought beer at the biker bars. Everyone always bought his. He was an arrogant misogynist. He looked at woman as objects of his pleasure, nothing more. I'd see him and say hello, shake his hand, and have small talk with him. I always seemed to make the guy laugh. I've always been a sociable person, so conversation was always easy. We'd tip glass beer bottles. Him drinking Bud Light and me drinking Lone Star Light. In the smoke-filled bar room, we'd cut up and laugh late into the night. I guess he took a liking to me. A liking to the point when I enter a beer joint, he'd call out from across the room, "Hey, Red." I turned my attention to the call of my voice to see him in a corner table behind six or eight empty beer bottles. I'd immediately walk to him and take a seat. He'd ask where I was coming from. It was usually another bar. He'd ask if it was dead or had a lot of people at it.

Sooner or later, someone would approach Chuck and greet him. They'd ask, "Are you ready for another, Chuck?"

He'd always say, "Sure, vato" (Spanish slang for dude), then he'd say, "And Red's ready for one too, vato. Hanging with Chuck started to have benefits. I wasn't spending as much on beer and people started giving me more respect because of whom I was sitting with.

After months of hanging out a lot. One day, Chuck asked me, "Hey, vato, how come you ain't in no club?"

I told him that I didn't see any that I thought were worth being in. There were lots of clubs that I thought had a lots of dorks as members. These were AMA clubs. I never gave a support club much thought because I didn't know any of the members.

He said, "What about a Bandido support club?"

At the time, there were the Southsiders MC and the Westsiders MC. I didn't live on either side of town. I lived on the northeast side of San Antonio. He said, "That don't matter, vato, you can still be in it."

I said, "Really?"

He said, "Sure, vato. Go with the Southsiders. Because their membership is low and they could use more members."

I knew Chuck knew what he was talking about. He had been a Bandido member since 1967.

I asked, "Well, how do I go about it?"

He said, "The next time you see a Southsider, approach him and tell him Chuck sent me to you."

Telling someone that was like saying the President of the United States sent me. At least in the motorcycle world, it did.

I came off IH-35 south and was traveling with a friend. His name was David Rodriguez. He was a Texas state prison guard. David would later in the years die in a motorcycle accident. It was a nice day in February 1996. South Texas has winter days that are like summer sometimes. That day was one of them. Now we came to a red light on the access road of IH-35 south and Ritterman Road. I asked David if he wanted to stop on Ritterman Road for a beer before we called it an afternoon. It was Sunday and we both had to work. He said no.

I said, "Are you sure?"

He said, "No, I gotta be going."

I said, "All right later," as our light turned green. I throttled my bikes and let out clutch as I waved goodbye to Dave once I took my hand off my clutch. I made my turn and continued my route in the direction of home. About a quarter mile down Ritterman, I saw a bar, Our Cocktails, which I'd been before and didn't like the atmosphere. Right next to it was where to next a bar I never had been in. It was a bar frequented by truck drivers from the area trucking companies. There were lots of trucking companies off Ritterman Road.

I pulled my bike in and parked. I took off my helmet and walked in. There behind the bar serving beer was the most gorgeous woman I had ever seen in my life. She was a Texas beauty. Shoulder-length blonde hair, blue eyes, the most beautiful face I'd ever seen on a woman. She had the most perfect figure. She was wearing Rocky Mountain white western shorts and Justin tennis shoes. Her skin was a golden bronze tan and her fingernails were manicured perfectly.

I walked up and asked for a Lone star Light as I kept my eyes fixated on her as she walked to the cooler and back to me. With a halfway laugh, she said, "$2.50 please" as if "What is your problem, buddy, what are you staring at?" I took my longneck and then I took a seat right at the bar. As I sat and sipped my beer not wanting to drink too fast because I was admiring her beauty. She looked in my direction, catching me staring time and time again. She'd give a courteous smile like "Are you ready for another beer?" She wasn't smiling like she was eating up me staring at her. This woman was drop dead gorgeous. I know she never lacked attention or compliments where ever she went.

When I did finish, I gestured, holding up my empty bottle as to get her attention. She walked toward me. I said, "I don't want to be rude, can I ask you your name so I don't have to say, hey, I need another beer?"

She said while continuing to smile, "My name is Diane."

I repeated it Diane, while thinking she probably heard that lame line a dozen time at this place.

I finished a couple of beers. Before walking out, I said, "Take it easy, Diane."

She replied, "Bye, thank you," as they do in most Texas business after you patronize the establishment.

Getting back on my bike, I rode off in the direction of my house, never knowing for a minute that Diane would be an answer to my prayer and that G-d would make her my wife.

Psalms 37:4 says, "Take delight in the LORD, and he will give you the desires of your heart."

I pulled into my driveway in the Sunrise Subdivision. The subdivision was dubbed GunRise because of all the shootings that happened in the neighborhood.

By the time I had my kickstand down and was taking off my helmet, I was greeted by Erika and Angel as always. Erika was nine and Angel was six at the time. Kristina was in transition of thinking she was thirteen going on twenty-one, so I wasn't daddy to her anymore; I was a dork.

I walked inside with Erika and Angel. I asked Kristina if anyone had called for me, she said no. I started one of my gourmet specialties, Hamburger Helper. After finishing and serving the girls, I went to my room because my head was pounding and my ears were ringing. I was nauseated and needed to lie down. I'd have these bouts of my ears ringing, feeling like throwing up, and excruciating headaches on the whole right side of my head to include my right eye.

A while later, my symptoms subsided and I decided to call Dave and tell him about the gorgeous woman I just saw hours earlier. I told him how so beautiful Diane was and how I planned to make it a regular daily stop.

In between time, I had to find a member of the Southsiders MC and approach him. While out on one of my evening cruises, I pulled into the Pour House Bar. The same place that I had met Kate at and where we talked about the scriptures and were having Christian fellowship. Most people would say how could you be Christian and be in a bar. I never claimed to be good at being a Christian because I wasn't. I was a bad example of one. I had been a bad example most of my life. Some might say G-d wouldn't be in a bar. Well, let me tell you he was and on more than one occasion. 1 Corinthians 1:27 says, "But G-d chose the foolish things of the world to shame the wise; G-d chose the weak things of the world to shame the strong." Whenever I least expected it, he was there. In a bar, in a store, on the street. He spoke through acquaintances, through movies, in church, through strangers, and when I read his word. G-d was everywhere and anywhere he wanted to be. Thank you, G-d, that you're not like man who will give up on someone and say that they're a hopeless case. No, G-d loves you with all his heart. His mercy lasts forever. His forgiveness has no end. If you blow it and mess things all up, all you have to do is drop to your knees and say, "G-d, I blew it and only Jesus can cleanse me from my sin."

I said hello to a couple of locals and then ordered my beer. About that time, someone had walked in the door. As he grabbed the door to keep the wind from slamming it against the outside brick wall, I saw the back of his cut (slang term for a vest with patches identifying the club you belong to). He turned in my direction. He had hair in a braid all the way down to his waist. He wore dark sunglasses; although the bar room lights were dimmed low, he didn't take them off. His shirt was a faded black Harley T-shirt from some dealership he must have visited. His jeans were faded and his boots well worn. The most distinctive thing about him was his long full beard that gave his appearance of someone who had Nordic ancestry. I mean, that was the first thing I noticed about him. His beard was so full and long, you couldn't see his mouth. He took a seat and lit a cigarette before his beer arrived. A Bud Light slides in front of him moments later. He exhaled his smoke and took a drink from the brown longneck bottle.

I got off my bar stool and walked halfway around the horse-shoe-shaped bar to where he was sitting. I glance up for a moment and my eye caught a glimpse of a fat bartender watching me as if I were about get myself in a bind for approaching this patch holder. With a cigarette hanging out of the bartender's mouth, he took a pull from it, making his hot box glow cherry red in the half-lit room. I walked up to this Viking bearded biker and asked if I could talk to him. His reply was huh as he looked over his dark sunglasses revealing only a small portion of his pupil, sclera, and iris. I repeated myself again, but this time, I said, "Chuck sent me." That caught his attention. He repeated Chuck and said, "Sure, what's up?"

I said, "How do I go about getting into the Southsiders MC? By the way, my name is Red."

He said, "My name is Joe but they call me Wyatt."

"Nice to meet you, Wyatt."

He mumbled half of something that I thought might have been "Same here. Well, you have to hang around, make the meetings, but you can't attend them. You can go with us to the functions we go to. The only catch is I have to talk to my president, and in the meeting, the club will discuss about letting you hang around."

I said, "Do you think you could do that for me?"

He said yeah and hit his cigarette. I said, "Thanks, I'll see you around" and went back to my bar stool. I told the bartender to give Wyatt a beer. I had not even given him my phone number or told him where I lived. It didn't matter because he wouldn't be looking for me. I'd have to find him if I wanted to get the answer the Southsiders would decide if I could hang with them or not.

The bartender fulfilled my request and Wyatt raised it in the above his head. The traditional way of saying thanks. I sat there thinking about Wyatt. He spoke real quiet. I wasn't sure if it was my hearing loss from my TBI or that was just the way he talked. If he did talk that quiet, he might consider changing his name from Wyatt to Whispers.

Me when I was four years old. I thought it was very bizarre and coincidental as a kid we got in the package of Fritos that mustache and that sticker and 30 years later I became a bandido.

This is me at Fort Leonard Wood Missouri
the back of a deuce and half

Basic training 1985

When I Graduated basic Training Fort Knox Kentucky
B Company 19th Battalion 4th training Brigade

US Army Air Assault Repelling Operation

US Army 101st Airborne Division Air Assault

Myself with my daughter Kristina while stationed
in Germany while in the US Army

Me at the Deer crossing Saloon in Selma, Texas

My first PRESIDENT and me

Myself with a member of the Outlaws MC

myself with a member of the Sons of Silence

Myself with some brothers and some Hells Angels

Myself surfing on my motorcycle

my cut that I wore for 10 years

the front of my cut

my cut at the time I retired from the club.

my Red brothers patch given to brothers with red hair

The charter member patch given at 10 years of membership

myself with a member of the Mongols MC

Myself with a member of the Pagans MC

Back of my new cut at the time of my retirement from the club

At the Deer crossing saloon

Myself while living in McQueeney, Texas

Me in my driveway in San Antonio on my fxd Super Glide

This is in 2001 when I first came into the
club riding through San Antonio

My visit to see the Romo's in Dallas 2018 I had not seen
them since I was 15 years old. Its been 37 years.

Myself in my ham Shack on my ham radio station today

Chapter 12

Now every day, I'd make a point of stopping into Where to Next to drink beer while Diane was on her shift. One night after a couple of months, I got the courage up to ask her for her phone number. She grabbed a bar napkin, and real fancy the way women write, she wrote her name and a phone number down. I said, "Thanks, can I call you?"

She said, "Well, would I have given you my number if I didn't want you to call?"

I said, "Oops, that was a dumb question. When should I call you?"

She said, "I'm off on Thursdays."

I said, "Okay, thanks."

It was Monday and I didn't want her to think I was being pushy so I didn't go into the bar the next three days. Thursday came as slow as it could come. I was really interested in Diane and was anxious to call her. It was around 4:30 p.m. when I dialed the phone number. On the other end, I heard a recording: "The number you have reached is not in service. Please check the number and dial it again."

I thought I must have dialed wrong so I looked at the napkin again and dialed it slowly so I wouldn't make a mistake. "The number you have reached is not in service. Please check the number and dial it again" came the recording again. Man, what a drag; she gave me fake number. I thought, Well, I can understand. As beautiful of a woman that she is, I bet she gets asked for her number all the time. She could have any man she wanted. She was drop dead gorgeous. I was just a regular dude. I wasn't the type of guy that women were throwing themselves at me. This woman was stunning. I guess I'm going to have work hard to earn her time. If I was ever going to be able to at all.

Well, Friday night came and I rode up to Where to Next. I walked in, and there she was beautiful as ever. Very nicely with a halfway chuckle, I said, "Hey, Diane, you gave me a fake number."

She got a kick out of it. She laughed and said, "I don't even know you or anything about you."

I said, "Well, how can you get to know me if I can't talk to you."

She said, "You can talk to me. You're taking to me right now," as she laughed.

I said, "It isn't the same. What do you want to know about me? I'll tell you anything you want to know. I work for the City of San Antonio, I have three daughters who I'm raising and I'm going through a divorce. Whooops, I should have never said that."

Diane said, "You're married."

I said, "No, I'm getting divorced."

She said, "You're married. Married is married and I don't date married men."

I was like "Ah, man, come on."

"Nope, married is married, Red." Then she gave me hope. She said, "When you're divorced, I will let you take me to lunch."

I said deal.

I rode off that evening, thinking, Now that's a respectable woman. The values her mother instilled in her were something you didn't see anymore. Especially in this "if it feels good, do it" world we live in.

The days and months passed and my divorce finally became final. I took my decree in my hand and headed for a phone booth. I called Diane's house. By then, we were talking on the phone. After talking to her at work for months, she figured there would be no harm in it. With that little bit of progress, I never even thought she might be interested in me. I was used to losing all my life.

I dialed her number and she picked up. I told her the divorce was final. She said I better not be lying or she wouldn't talk to me again. I told her I'd bring it and show her in person. So I went to her house after she gave me the address. I knocked on the door and a skinny young boy answered the door, wearing starched Wranglers, a t-shirt, and baseball cap. With a halfway cocky voice, he said, "Yeah."

I said, "Is Diane home?"

He looked me up and down and walked off without saying a word. I could hear his muffled voice telling his mom, "There's some guy at the door asking for you."

I had just met Jason, Diane's seventeen-year-old son. She came to the door halfway hiding behind it with her bath robe on. I said, "Are you ready for lunch?"

She laughed and said, "I'm not going today."

I pleaded, "I've waited months for this moment."

She told me, "Well, you're going to wait longer. You call me and ask me out properly."

I complied and said, "Okay, can I call you tonight?"

She told me yes and I said my goodbye to her. As I drove off again, it came to mind. Wow, her mother sure raised her proper. She was a lady and I was going to have to ask her out the right way like a gentleman. I liked that quality in her. She was definitely a respectable lady.

About a week later, she accepted my invitation to lunch. Diane had a daytime job and wasn't working at the bar very much at all. She was an assistant book keeper for a local construction contractor. During the day at work, I pretty much had free roam of the northeast side of the city because of all the parks on that side of town. So we met at Wendy's where she wanted to go because she said she loved their salads. I got a cheeseburger and fries. We talked about different things. Time flew as it always does when you don't want it to and it was time to go back to work. I thanked Diane for going to lunch with me. We said goodbye. I told her I would call her later.

Chapter 13

ithin a few weeks of talking with Wyatt again, the club he belonged to, the Southsiders MC, had voted and agreed to start letting me be a hang around (a person seeking to prospect in a motorcycle club). So week after week, I would contact different members of the Southsiders. There was Eric, Gilbert, Jack, Lester, and of course, Wyatt.

Not long after I started hanging around, Wyatt retired from the Southsiders and I didn't see him again. Week after week, month after month, I went to bars, motorcycle rallies, house parties, and anything else the Southsiders did. I wanted in and I was dedicating myself. Four months had passed and I was beginning to get discouraged. I had now also started a relationship with Diane. We saw each other daily and our children and us did thing together. Jason had turned eighteen and had moved out, but Diane had her twin daughters, Danica and Danielle, still at home. My two younger girls, Erika and Angel, loved playing with Danica and Danielle while Diane and I watched TV and talked. My oldest daughter, Kristina, was at the age in her life when your child thinks that hanging out with you is for the birds. She rarely gave me the time of day because she was a typical teenager on the phone and all. All the girls never wanted for the evenings to end. Danica and Danielle never wanted myself, Erika, and Angel to go home. Now Diane was a G-dsend to me and I was too dumb to even know that G-d's blessing was before me. We eventfully moved in together at my house. Diane would cook dinner, clean the house, wash our laundry, but most of all, she was being a mother to my children. She included them in everything she did. If she bought clothes for Danica and Danielle, she would get Krissy,

Erika, and Angel the same. Like I said, G-d had sent this woman to me and I was too dumb to realize it. My mind was on membership in the Southsiders MC. Now most might think that living together wasn't right. Correct, it wasn't. Diane didn't know Jesus as Lord and Savior. I wasn't living as the Christian that I was supposed to be either. There is hope with almighty G-d. He had plans for Diane and me. It was in the future. I'm glad G-d isn't like us. We look for the fault in each other. G-d looks at a broken person and says, "I can do wonders with him or her." Or in our case both of us.

The time had come one evening. The Southsiders were having their weekly meeting and like for the last five months I was in attendance. We were at Rhonda's Roadhouse on Nagalitos Street in San Antonio, Texas. They sent Lester to get me from the barroom. They called me into their meeting and said, "You've been hanging around for months now. We were wondering if you were interested in prospecting for the Southsiders."

I said, "Yes, I want to very bad."

I was told to leave the area of the bar where they were conducting their club business. A few minutes later, Lester motioned with his hand for me to come back around the bar where all the members were at. They said you need a sponsor (sponsor, an individual responsible for your actions and helping teach you how to carry yourself as a member). Is anyone willing to sponsor Red? With a heavy Spanish accent, Gilbert said he would be my sponsor. Eric was the president and said okay, give him a prospect patch. It was gold letters on a red background the reverse way the Bandidos had their colors. The colors were reversed because the Bandidos didn't want anyone trying to imitate them. I only received the top rocker. The rest of the patch would be given to you if you made it.

I was instructed to go find a bar table, sew the prospect patch on my vest, and come back. I finished sewing and returned like I was told. The meeting adjourned and Jack cussed at me and told me to go with him. We mounted our Harleys and we took off tires smoking. Exceeding the speed limit, we raced down Malone Street toward Jack's House on the south side of San Antonio. But first, we stopped for four cases of beer. Jack loved to drink Bud Light. I was given the task of carrying all this beer. I was a prospect and Jack earned his patch a long time ago. So he wasn't going to carry any of the beer. I was a prospect. Beneath him and every other patch holder. Like a pledge in a college fraternity, I was at the disposal of the Southsiders and any Bandido that wanted to use me for club business.

We got to his house and went into the garage where there was a refrigerator. He ordered me to fill it with the beer he had just bought. Jack was no-nonsense kind of guy. He was only about 5'5" but was a solid 175 pounds at least. As you can imagine, for his height, most would be 140 pounds. But he wasn't fat. He was solid and strong. He wore a baseball cap, had a thin red mixed with black mustache and a thin goatee. A T-shirt, his vest of course, Levi jeans, and exotic skin cowboy boots. Full quill ostrich if I remember correctly. Red facial hair and a white completion indicated to me Spaniard blood. Indigenous Indians of Mexico and South American did not have matching traits. Just like myself, thus the reason for being given the nickname Red.

He had big custom gold rings on all his fingers. These rings served as brass knuckles when he knocked you out. Brass knuckles without them being illegal. He knew how to use them and he would use them if he felt you disrespected him, our club, or his wife. Jack's wife Ava was a very beautiful Mexican woman. She was petite, with long black straight hair. He was very protective of her along with be very jealous. She was a very nice respectable woman. She was always hospitable to me whenever I came to their house. Offering me something to drink or something to eat. Her and Jack would even let me camp out on their couch if I had too many beers. Myself and Jack in the future would become very close to each other. We shared lots of laughs. We had lots of fun traveling the United States on motorcycles. He took very good care of me whenever I was drunk. He always looked out for me in a protective way. Making sure I had a ride home so I wouldn't ride my motorcycle drunk and get killed. I appreciate him very much for always looking out for me the way that he always did.

Prospecting is very hard physically and mentally. The mental part was nothing. I survived basic training. Sleep depredation was very hard on me because I worked a full-time job.

Day after day and month after month, I was like a slave to the club. After about three months, I earned my full patch in the Southsiders MC. I noticed when earning my full patch, a lot of clout came with it. All the other independent riders and AMA clubs respected you. They wanted to buy your beer and do favors to get on your good side.

I've always loved people and I rarely took advantage of this new opportunity. MC living was a lifestyle. It was very demanding. I neglected my daughters and future wife Diane. This woman never gave up on me. I've always have had a problem with love. Not romantic love but feeling loved. I guess it is rooted in me from my childhood. Deep inside, I yearned for acceptance and love, but it just wasn't there. G-d loved me dearly also, but I was too busy trying to win love from the world.

I traveled across the United States on my motorcycle with the club. All over the United States. Miles and miles of highway under the protection of G-d. You never realize it when you are running wild and sinning along the way. G-d is the furthest from your mind. I spent many nights and some days in the bars of San Antonio. Laughing it up, drinking Lone Star beer. When the party ended, I would make my solo journey back home to find my entire household sound to sleep. Most women would have bailed on a man, but Diane always stood by me. For what, I don't know. I know now, because G-d answered my prayers for a good wife with her. She's the best as they come. She is such a gorgeous woman and could have the attention of any man. She didn't need me. G-d knew I needed her in my life after the pain I went through with my first marriage. We didn't have a perfect relationship. We had our ups and downs. Time and time again, I thought she was through with me, but she loved me and stayed with me anyway.

I had a quality in me I never knew existed. I was a great salesman. I eventually became the secretary of the Southsiders. We had a few items we'd sell to offset our travel costs when we'd go on our runs. Stickers and other items that said "Support your Local Southsiders MC."

Like usual people wanted them to try and get close to you and be friends with you. So they'd buy whatever I had. Now I'll try to explain this. I hope you can understand. I am not a salesman. You see something happens in my mind after my TBI. My mind will not turn off. If I start something, I have to continue until it's complete. So I would sell the support items and completely sell them out. My fellow members noticed and they were very pleased. To me, I was receiving the love of acceptance that I wanted from people. This continued on for some time.

The Bandidos soon took notice to my ability also. You know the way I could sell things. I was approached by the San Antonio Chapter secretary. He asked if I could help sell their support items. Shirts, stickers, cozies, posters, and ash trays. I said sure. I wanted acceptance from the Bandidos. They were running Texas in the motorcycle world. So what better way to get close to them than to sell their support stuff. There would be times my club would tell me to be somewhere and the sergeant at arms C. H. would say, "Tell Eric to call me." I'd do what I was told, and about five minutes later, Eric would say go ahead to the San Antonio Chapter's meeting.

While I was conducting business for the San Antonio Chapter. Making the meetings of my club running the bars getting drunk and all. I heard rumor that the San Antonio Chapter was going to Probate some of the Support Club members. Man, what a dream come true to be able to become a Bandido.

The chapter secretary one night asked me at the bar. "Red, how long have you been in your club?"

I said, "Almost two years."

He said, "Man, if you had two years, you come with us."

Wow, I couldn't believe what he just said. Man, I thought I would love to become a Bandido.

Jack and Gilbert left my club and became Probate Bandidos. The Bandidos did in fact select some support members to probate into their chapter. They got to wear the Fat Mexican patch. With Bandidos top rocker and the bottom rocker that read probationary. The bottom rocker was letting the Bandido Nation and all others know they were going to be full members one day. I would watch Jack and other probationary members sport their cut. Man, it was awesome. I couldn't wait until my time came. Surely, the secretary would put in a good word for me. I'd be able to make the jump for sure. Not every support club member was approached by the Bandidos to probate for them. They had to be interested in you and have a quality in you that appealed to them. Mine was because I was a salesman. I could generate revenue by selling t-shirts, stickers, cozies, and other stuff with their name on it.

The time came as my time elapsed and I started to hint to the secretary about helping me make the move up. He said he'd bring it up in the meetings they had. Well, growing impatient as I have always been, I started asking him about it. He said they were going to discuss it.

Jealousy and envy are a part of any organization. You have those who think you're great but then there are others who just don't like you. I soon learned that there were members who didn't want me in the San Antonio chapter. For no other reason than that they just didn't like me. They didn't have to have a reason. They were Bandidos. They were brothers. Like we used to say, and I wasn't nothing. As Bandidos, they would say, "Your brother may not always be right, but he is always your brother." So it didn't matter and I didn't matter. With that, my dream of becoming a Bandido would never happen. I continued riding with the Southsiders.

Little did I know there was a chapter watching me all along. They recognized my selling ability. It was the Hill County Chapter. It was ran by German guy. He went by three names. I heard different people call him one of the three names. David was his vice president. David would later become such a good friend and a born-again Christian. It's amazing what G-d can do with a man's heart.

I remember hearing the Hill Country President tell David, "We neet to bring dis guy in before dey change dare mind und another chapter gets him." The Hill Country Chapter president was German and had a strong German accent. David agreed and began inviting me to their meetings. He was the chapter's vice president and I would always hear from him about what was going on with their chapter. David would let me know what was going on, where they were going to be at so I could hook up with the chapter.

It was the same thing as before hanging out to prove yourself worthy. Showing them what you are about. I put in more long nights and days. More time away from my family like before. I had to do this. I had to be somebody. My whole life I've been a failure. If I wasn't careful, my mother's words would come true and I would never amount to anything. I had to do this, I kept telling myself. I was going to stick it out. No matter how long it would take.

One night, we were in Natalia. Natalia is one of many small towns south of San Antonio. The Hill Country chapter was holding their weekly meeting. Of course, I was in attendance, but not allowed into the meeting itself because I wasn't a member yet.

Suddenly, I was called into the bar. Anyone who wasn't a member of the chapter had to wait outside the bar. I complied and waked fast to the entrance of a local bar and grill. Inside, Bandidos were lounging around the room. I glanced for a second at each member not holding my eyes on any of them too long. I didn't want to show any disrespect. I was asked by the president and the VP as the other members looked on. Various questions. "Are you sure you want this? Are you sure you can handle it? Have you told your family what you are about to do?| I answered yes to all their questions. The president said, "You're about to step out of your world and into ours."

In my mind I said okay, I've seen all the fun you have and I want in. Never once thinking about sixteen years prior how I surrendered my life to Christ and wanted to follow him. I had put Christ on the back burner of my life. Not remembering anything except wanting that patch all of them wore.

I snapped back to reality when a shirt was thrown at me. It was a T-shirt that had the Bandidos name and some other stuff on it. I lit up like a light. I had just gained membership in the Bandidos Motorcycle Club. I was a probationary member of the Hill Country Chapter.

I looked down with a smile and kept staring at the shirt. Still in shock of what had just happened. When all of a sudden, a big Bandido, a big Mexican, tall and broad shouldered, yelled at me with a halfway smile the way that brother always smiled. He said, "Put that shirt on. Hurry up, get that other shirt off before we change our mind."

As the bar cheered me on, I took off my Harley Davidson T-shirt and quickly put on the shirt that announced to the world who had just taken me in and who I had just become.

I would now live by the following creed. Now and when I finally received my Texas bottom rocker.

Bandidos 1%ER

A 1%ER is the (1%) of one hundred of us who have given up on society and the politicians' one way law. This is why we look repulsive to you. So stay out of our face. Look at your brother standing next to you and ask yourself if you would give him half of what's in your pocket or half of what you have to eat. If a citizen hits your brother, will you be on him without asking why? There is no why. Your brother may not be right, but he is always your brother. It's one for all of us and all of us for one. If you don't think this way, then walk away. Because you are a citizen and you don't belong here with us. We are the Bandidos. Members will follow the Bandidos way or get out. All members are your brothers and your family. You will not steal your brother's possessions, money, woman, class, or his humor. If you do this, your brothers will do you.

B.F.F.B

(Bandidos Forever Forever Bandidos)

Chapter 14

After celebrating with all my new soon-to-be brothers. Downing beer, smoking Marlboro cigarettes, and cutting up through the night. The night came to an end and I headed home on my bike. I was ecstatic all the way home. As I rode into the night, I kept thinking, I did it I was in. What I had dreamed about for years finally came true. I thought I would wake up and find out I was dreaming. It was no dream. It had really happened. I was somebody now. The world would know me as Bandido Texas Red. The respect would be given by all who came into my presence that didn't wear our patch.

The probationary period in the Bandidos is different than prospecting. With a probationary period, it was typically a year. It could be longer or shorter, it depended on you and your president. You had to prove yourself and the chapter would make a decision when you would get your Texas bottom rocker. It would take a 100 percent vote by all members of the chapter. As like in our country's government, the president of the chapter had the final say-so. He could object and override the vote of the rest of the members.

I would display my cut with pride. I wore it at all the bars. Everyone I saw would approach me with caution as not to show any disrespect to those colors. They all feared all the repercussion that they knew would happen if they did. But I was never like that. I treated everyone the same. The same as before. With respect and dignity as human beings should show each other.

We are made in the image of G-d. G-d is a spirit and the spirits that are in us are like G-d. In the aspect of his likeness. Not equal. Never could we be equal to G-d. G-d is not a respecter of men. Acts 10:34 says, "We are equal to each other. G-d loves us all equal."

Even in our disobedience, he continues to love us. As a father, I love all my children. They have no idea how much I do. The same is with G-d; we have no idea how much he loves us. Our love even as much as we love will never equal to his. Why do I say this because I know I could never send one of my children to die on a cross. Let alone, my only son. They way G-d did for us.

Lucifer was jealous and wanted to be like G-d. He wanted to be equal to G-d. He was cast down by G-d. G-d transformed him into the devil and created hell for him and his angels. His only mission is to destroy us. He hates us because G-d loves us. G-d loves us and sent his son Jesus to the cross to die for us. For all of our sins.

The sinful life I had lived and even though I turned my back on G-d, he still loved me. He never gave up on me. He waited for my return. Loving me even though I had forgotten all about him. I was bought with a price, with that price you are his forever. No matter how many times you blow it, G-d says, "You are still mine. I still love you. If you get on your knees and ask my forgiveness, I will surely forgive you."

Everyone was comfortable around me. They knew the same Red had not changed because he was wearing a Bandido patch. AMA club members as well as independent riders would all associate with me. They weren't on edge because they knew I was a friendly guy.

Chapter 15

I t was a great feeling riding with the chapter. A large pack of brothers going down the highway. The open road, the feeling of freedom. Watching the people in the cars as we roared by them. Pointing with wide eyes recognizing the Outlaw patch that put fear in people because of the reputation it had. This was an Outlaw motorcycle club. If you knew about it, that was good. If you didn't, you very well might find out the hard way real fast. With a smashing fist to your jaw by one of the brothers. It would forever remind you of what that patch meant. You wouldn't make the same mistake of disrespect ever again.

I hadn't been in the club but about a few months. We had a meeting at the Lucky Lady Saloon off of IH-35 south before Lytle. It was a dump ran by a local San Antonio guy named Work Horse. His real name was Edmond. I never seen him ride a Harley, but for some reason, he was always around the scene. Kind of like Albert and the Ghost Riders, a local San Antonio band. They'd play in biker bars we went to around the San Antonio Area. Needless to say, the Lucky Lady wasn't so lucky, and neither was Work Horse. The bar went out of business a couple of months after it opened.

I heard some time later in the years, Work Horse died. When they told me he died, I said really? As you do every time they say someone died. My mind had drifted. I thought I wonder if Edmond knew Jesus. I was snapped back to where I was when I heard, "Hey, we're pulling out and heading to another bar." I donned my full-face helmet and saddled up on my FXD. Simultaneously hitting the electric starter button as I raised my kickstand. As the road captain pulled out into the road to stop traffic, everyone roared out of the parking lot. I looked in my rearview mirror to catch a glimpse of the road captain's image getting bigger until he passed me and returned to his spot with the rest of the chapter officers in the front of the pack.

I remember the night as if it were yesterday. I stopped into Tiffany's pool hall on San Pedro Street. Just an hour before my chapter brothers had broke off and went their own way. Some maybe went home, others went to different bars, I guess. I only thought that because I usually went to another bar before going home for the night.

Some members of the SWSA chapter were there drinking as I entered Tiffany's. I greeted my brothers from the SWSA chapter with hugs and firm pats on the back. The unique sound of a hand slapping against leather echoed loudly showed that you cared for each other.

I gestured to the waitress by pointing my index finger in the air. She approached me and took my order of a Lone Star Light. Returning quickly to deliver the cold beverage of hops and barley to ensure she received her tip.

I sat down next to James. He was from the west side of San Antonio in the Loma Park area. With a smile, he told me to pull up a bar stool. I did and we began to visit. Neither one of us knew it would be the last time we talked. We were shooting the bull. I can't even remember what we were talking about. It didn't matter because no conversation was more as important than if James knew Jesus Christ. Within an hour or so of me leaving that night, James would be whirled into eternity; ready or not, our L-rd would call him home.

Chapter 16

I carried a pager and a cell phone back then. Cell phones were just starting to come around and were expensive to have. I managed to be able to afford one. I wanted to look important so I carried a cell and a pager.

No matter how drunk I would get, I always woke up early. From the time in the army to the everyday grind of my City of San Antonio job, it was programmed into me. I woke up. The girls and Diane were still asleep, so like a ninja, I made my way to the living room after slipping on my jeans. I didn't even get a cup of joe as my attention was drawn to my pager. I glanced at it to see a familiar number. It was Peter from my chapter. After his number, there were three other numbers: 911. It was our code for call back it's important. Immediately I did as I walked barefoot out the front door in my jeans and into the concrete driveway. Peter was also a working stiff so I knew it wasn't too early to call him back. As the sound of the phone ringing against my ear, within a few rings, I heard Peter answer, "Hello."

I said, "What's up, Peter?"

He said, "Did you hear about last night?"

I said, "No, what's up?"

He said, "They killed James last night at Tiffany's."

I froze for a moment. Without words, looking for the right thing to say, I muttered, "Man, I was talking to him last night."

Peter said, "You were?"

I said, "Yes, I went there after I left the Lucky Lady."

Peter and I both expressed that we couldn't believe that James was gone. Our call ended. I hung up and walked back inside. Looking for solace as I walked back into the house, Diane was up and asked who I was talking to. I said, "Peter said someone killed James last night."

She covered her mouth with her hand in silence for a moment and then asked me all the questions a person would ask. As I sat with my head hung, I said, "I didn't know yet. They said someone shot him in the bar." I felt so bad for James. I thought about his wife. How she must have been going out of her mind. Then I thought how G-d had directed me home out of harm's way. I hadn't been in the Bandidos very long and already someone I knew had been killed.

Did it stop me, no? I continued being a Bandido. I was a man; nothing would stop me from being a man. I rode hard. Like I said before, the party never stops and the highway never ends. Not once did I take in consideration that G-d kept me from harm's way. Like the prodigal son, I continued my riotous living.

Chapter 17

Now Ray and I were friends before we ever became Bandidos. We would ride our Harleys all over town. I don't recall how we met. I'm sure it was in some biker bar in San Antonio where I met most of the people I knew. Ray is what I used to call him. I always got along with him. He always had a sinister smile on his face. I know many will find it hard to believe when I say he was always cool with me. He seemed to like me. I can't say anything bad about him because he always treated me right. He was a killer. I never knew it because he didn't advertise it. He was a stand-up dude. What I mean by that, he'd stand and fight no matter what.

One night, I was in Rhonda's Road House on Nogolitos Street in San Antonio. The same bar I got prospected in for the Southsiders. A guy broke a longneck on Ray's face. Blood was gushing from his head. Immediately, patrons from the bar split the fight up. I was playing pool and saw it happen from across the room. I went closer to see what was happening. A large crowd had formed so I could only see from the back of the crowd. There was Ray with the smile he always had, telling everyone to let them both go with a big smile on his face. The bar owner made Ray and the other guy leave the bar because the police were on their way. Ray later on became a member of the Macheteros MC. It was a Bandido support club like the Southsiders. The Macheteros hadn't been around very long. Ray was one of the original members. He got into the Macheteros a few months after I became a Southsider.

I would later come to find out in the years to come that Ray had killed his girlfriend's dad, the person who killed Bandido James, and later he would kill a world champion boxer. Never in my life would

I had thought Ray was capable of doing any of this. You would have never known he was capable of it. Well hey, that's what they always say, right? When you see neighbors interviewed about a killer. They say he was always friendly, a quiet guy. I mean Ray wasn't quiet, he was outgoing. He was friendly only to you if you were his friend. I think for the most part, he tolerated most people.

In the first year, there was a lot of death around me. After James was killed, another Bandido named Big Ray was killed in San Antonio by a gunman trying to steal his motorcycle as he worked on it on the side of the road. When they attempted to steal it, he stood up to them. When they couldn't beat him, they shot him and he died. I didn't get a chance to get to know Big Ray. He was prospecting while I was probating. The few times I spoke with him, he seemed to be a stand-up guy. It's a shame he lost his life.

In the first year in the club, I attended fourteen funerals across the United States. Most died from motorcycle accidents and some from sickness. If you were within 500 miles of the brother that died, it was mandatory to attend the funeral.

The funerals were like nothing you ever seen. Hundreds of Bandidos all wearing the same patch. The bottom rocker told where they traveled from. It wasn't unusual to see one from Europe or Australia. It was the greatest respect you could receive as a member. To be given a Bandido funeral. All your brothers coming to bury you. I truly mean bury you. We would form two lines across from each other from the hearse to the plot. Every member would pass the brother's casket down the line to the plot.

The brother would be eulogized and then lowed into the ground to their eternally rest. Shovels then were passed out and every member in attendance took turns. Everyone shoveled dirt into the grave, handing a shovel to the next brother and then the next. Each Bandido took their turn doing this until the casket showed no more. Ashes to Ashes Dust to Dust.

Genesis 3:19 says, "In the sweat of thy face shalt thou eat bread, till thou return unto the ground; for out of it wast thou taken: for dust thou art, and unto dust shalt thou return."

The brothers were very close to me, so naturally, it caused me grief to see them go. Never knowing if in a week, month or a year, would it be me they were passing to my plot. G-d had encamped his angels around me and protected me. I don't know why. I wasn't living for him, I was living for myself, I was living for the world. He was always merciful to me. G-d knows every man's heart. I think the only reason G-d protected me was because he knew my heart. I was unworthy of his love, but he loved me anyway.

Riding with the club took me from city to city, town to town, and state to state. I've been places I will never see again. I meet people I would never see again. Little southern towns of Texas, New Mexico, Louisiana. Well, I traveled a lot. I had been to Alabama, Louisiana, all over Texas, Arizona, Colorado, Utah, Kansas, Nebraska, Wyoming, and South Dakota on my motorcycle. I traveled to California, Nevada, and Washington different times while in the club but not on my bike. Traveling by airplane to attend Bandido parties out of state.

You know everyone is created by G-d. He loves all of us. Most who know me knew that I professed Jesus Christ. They all knew that I wasn't ashamed of Jesus Christ. Sure, I got laughed at and ridiculed from time to time. Sometimes, I'd get deep in conversation with some brothers as G-d's word would come up in conversation.

Some brothers were very receptive to my fellowship of the word. Heck, there was a full member from Austin. He was a bona fide preacher. You see, contrary to what authorities might have you believe that all Bandidos were drug dealers, pimps, and gun runners, it wasn't the case. In fact, more San Antonio Police officers were arrested than Bandidos were in all the years I was in the club. The news never covered those cases the way they did the Bandidos.

These guys were my brothers. No matter what propaganda rises, most were lies. My brothers worked regular jobs, owned legitimate businesses, had families, wives, children, and grandchildren just like anyone else. Now granted they aren't the Boy Scouts. They never claimed to be.

It hurts to see some of these brothers go down. If there was only something I could have said or done. The guilt always plagued me in my mind. I let my G-d down. I let my brothers down. I could have shared his love and word with more of the brothers. Instead, I just stood by and downed my beer with them.

I want G-d to forgive me because I could have done more. I should have said more. People liked me. I made brothers laugh. They knew they could confide in me if they needed to. So many brothers that would die and so many others I saw go to prison. I sometimes did as the Lord commanded me to as a Christian. I would write them. Some I would travel to visit in prison. I would go as often as I could. I would write a lot of letters. It wasn't enough I could have done more. It hurts me to see some of these brothers with their entire life destroyed by the enemy. Most I will never see again.

Chapter 18

The Hill Country chapter got the word from our national chapter that a long-time member named Jake from the Dallas Area had died of a heart attack. David, by that time, was our chapter president. The president had become a national sergeant at arms. As the chapter secretary, I was e-mailed about Jake's death and details of the funeral. It was my job to immediately to inform David about the tragic news. At our weekly meeting, I addressed the chapter and give details of the meeting time and the route our chapter would take to Dallas. The rest of the members would make plans to make the road trip to the funeral. The Hill Country chapter had a brother who had recently transferred from the El Paso chapter to the Hill Country chapter because of work. His name was Bob. He was thin about 5'7". He wore glasses some-time to read I think. He had face hair that reminded me of Robert Gould Shaw. A colonel in the Union army during the Civil War. He had a collection of knives and swords from the Civil War era and some other American conflicts. Most of his collection were post–Civil War. He loved coffee. We'd sit and drink it. Whenever me, David, and him would meet up, it was for sure a cup of Joe was going to be drank by all of us.

We set out for Dallas late one afternoon for Jake's funeral. From the point where we met up, we all roared out in formations, switching the gears on the iron machines that we rode. Like futuristic cowboys, we traveled up IH-35 North. It was probably traveled by cowboys of Texas a hundred years before us. Only they would be riding horses and driving stagecoaches. One could imagine the David Mann art-work of Ghost Rider. It was a ghost of a cowboy riding above in the distance of a desert road next to a long-haired biker who had no inclination that he was there.

As we rode many times down the highways and byways, I would drift off into my thoughts like I always did. The same way that I would like when I was a young boy back in Wisconsin. Sometimes, they were fantasies that I was in my own world, nobody or nothing to get in my way. Sometimes, I would miss my dad dearly. I missed him so bad. How would he think of me? Me being part of an Outlaw motorcycle club. Feared by everyone who seen us. I would imagine trying to explain to my dad how good these guys were. Ah, but it was all a daydream; he had died in 1995 as I was brought back to the highway again of downshifting motors and the vision of turn signals coming on one after another, indicating we were leaving the highway to ride along the access road.

We pulled off to meet the intersection of the access road and Walnut Street in New Braunsfel, Texas. A small city about fifteen miles or so from San Antonio. New Braunsfel is the same town that the Sutherland Spring church shooter lived in. We stopped to wait on the red light. Within moments of stopping, it seemed to turned green. First gear letting out the clutch as we crossed the intersection and braking again to pull into the McDonalds next to the Exxon on our right. Everyone backed into a space all next to each other. Backing in always ensured a quick easy departure when we finished our Big Mac value meals or whatever you got. It was also a way of nobody being able to read your license plate number. I sat down with my cup of coffee as Bob came into view in the dining room. Soon, David joined us. Lester and Lou passed by as Lester teased Lou for ordering the biggest order on the menu. Lester and Lou were road dogs. They were roommates when I first met them. They were good friends prior to coming into the club. They even prospected together. Other members joined the chapter after getting what they were going to eat.

As I sat with Bob, G-d came up in the conversation. Bob had told me that he was a saved Christian. He had accepted Christ as his Lord and Savior. The conversation was great. I let him know I had received Christ back in 1985 in Kentucky while in US Army basic training. We fellowshipped until it was time to hit the road again. I threw my coffee cup in the trash, exited the restaurant, and approached my bike. Bikes fired up one after the other. We all donned our full-face helmets. Kickstands up and the road captain pulled into the access road to guard the lane from oncoming traffic as David led the way. To the right then switching to the left lane and up the entrance ramp back on IH-35 north. Never knowing what was in store for us just a few miles up the highway. For a moment, I was hoping the coffee would not go through me as it always did. It had a tendency to do that, prompting me to make a stop to use the latrine.

I don't remember what I was thinking about. We were all in the hammer lane when I started to see that our lane was going to end. More frightening than that was a semi truck was on our right leaving us nowhere to go. I pulled my throttle as far back as it would go. I downshifted and throttled again. Knowing I had to beat the eighteen-wheeler before the road ran out. I passed it and looked in my rearview mirror to see David make it, and all of a sudden, I saw bikes sliding in the grass then one flipped over and over again. I looked in horror. As I pulled fast as I could to the very right of the high way. I waited until I knew I could cross back safely. I blasted across all the lanes and began flying as fast as I could toward the oncoming traffic. As horns from vehicles blared as I passed them in the wrong direction. I finally saw a couple of prospects lying in the grass. I stopped for a split second asking if they were okay. With a head shake, they indicated yes. I blasted up to Lou who was also lying on the ground. He was okay also. He was smiling. Maybe he was shocked that he didn't die.

I proceeded to the next bike and its rider; it was Bob. He was lying motionless in the grass. I lifted his break-away jaw on his full face. I was thinking his face would reveal him in pain. My heart dropped as there was no life in him. I denied it by calling his name over and over. I tried to lift him by the front of his vest. Just then David was behind me. When lifted Bob up so far, blood began to pour out of his mouth. I gently lowered him back down to his original position. I began to lament. David was lamenting too. This was a brother who not twenty minutes ago was drinking coffee with me talking about Jesus Christ. I could not believe he was gone. The breath of life that G-d breathed into Bob at the time of his birth was the same breath of life that G-d had just taken back. Bob was gone to eternity. Soon the familiar sight of red and blue strobe lights came into view brighter and brighter as they drew closer to us. I didn't see them load Bob up. The New Braunsfel Police began asking me details of what had ensued. The semi truck never stopped. Nobody driving behind us offered help. Nobody ever stopped the truck driver. Surely being that I saw the motorcycles crashing many others had to see what had transpired. Nobody ever came forth.

We never made it to Dallas that day. With Bob deceased and others on the way to the hospital, the ones who weren't injured went back home. David contacted Bob's family to give them the tragic news. Later on, I got a call from a Nomad. He was probably born around the year of my dad I'm guessing. I don't know for sure. He said, "Oh man, brother, I'm glad you answered. Are you okay?"

"Yes," I said.

He said he heard that a member was killed from my chapter on the way to the funeral in Dallas. He asked if another Nomad member who use to be around the Hill Country chapter often was okay also. Being that the other Nomad was usually around our chapter, he assumed he was with us. I said no, he wasn't with us.

I felt a little consoled that brother was checking on me. Like I said before, they try to make the Bandidos out to be all bad, but I know different. I felt that at least someone cared in my time of grief. They care enough to see if I was alive. That tells me that as a brother and a friend that brother cared enough to see that I was okay. We had all just lost a brother in our chapter. Bandido Bob wore a patch just like most of us wore. It read gone but not forgotten. The brother was now riding in the forever chapter. The forever chapter makes reference to them riding with brothers that had died before them.

Chapter 19

Funeral arrangements would have to made for Bob. After a while, the Holy Spirit gave me comfort knowing my friend would have eternal life. He indeed knew Jesus Christ as his Savior.

He was buried in Kerrville, Texas, out in the Texas Hill Country. As any Bandido funeral, brothers from everywhere came to conduct the ritual I had come to know so often. Besides Bandido members, AMA clubs, Mom and Pop clubs, and riding clubs, independent riders would also attend these Bandido funerals.

After as always, we would hit a local bar and drink. Smoke-filled bar rooms, laughter, and the muffled sounds of conversations barely heard over the blare of jukebox music. We would all visit with all the out-of-town brothers into the late night. Some would leave right after the funeral, but most would hang in the bar.

Offers of lodging at other local members' houses were always offered and almost always accepted. Some of these brothers had very long ways to go to get back to where they lived. So an offer of a sofa was always eagerly accepted. It was always good to get a good night's rest before starting a long road trip home. I would always accept an offer from an out-of-town brother when I was far from my home.

Sometimes, I would go back to a chapter brother's house also and continue the conversations that we had at the bar we had just left. Great hospitality was always shown to the out-of-town brothers. They were always treated like kings. Our brotherhood prided ourselves on this. After all, we called ourselves brothers. Brothers from another mother is what I would say. In my opinion, we treated each other better than biological family would treat each other most of the time. Even if a brother's mother or father died, all the local Bandidos would pull into the parking lot of the funeral home. The parking lot was full of Bandidos. All of us were there to show that brother that we all cared that his mother had passed away. Never going into funeral home. Everyone always stayed in the parking lot together.

This life had consumed my everyday living. Putting the club first always showed that you were a good brother, a good Bandido. Even at the expense of our loved ones.

I saw many marriages/relationships end because individuals were so involved in the club. Family neglected. Jobs were lost. Everything and anything was second to the club. I did my fair share of neglecting Diane and our children. It caused big problems in my relationship with Diane. We would argue a whole lot. No matter how much we argued, Diane never gave up on me. She let me keep being a man. What I considered being a man was all about. With the Bandidos, I was accepted. I was cared about. A way I never was cared about as a child. The only place other than in the Bandidos motorcycle club that I felt this camaraderie was in the army. There were plenty of veterans in the Bandidos. I know they felt the same way as I did. It was the closest thing to being in the military. This is the reason I think so many veterans would seek out membership in the club.

Sure, my father always showed he loved me and I knew he did. He never said it much, but it was there in his actions. Like I have said before, I heard that actions speak louder than words. That is true. I also heard it said before there are people who love you so much, they just don't know how to say it. My dad was one of them and it was something I had learned from him. I loved my children with all my being. I just didn't know how to say it. I'm not blaming my dad. He was the best. I love and miss him every day. But you learn things and it was something I learned. To say I love my children is something I regret not saying often.

If I say I loved them it was like this. I would say, "You know I love you and your sisters very much." I would never direct it to them as individuals. I would never say, "I love you very much. You are my daughter and I love you." I'm ashamed that I would tell them directly. Even the twins. I tell them the same thing. "I love you like my daughter. I know I'm not your father, but I still love you like you are one of my daughters." I don't know what was buried deep inside of me. Why I couldn't bring myself to just say it. Maybe I was afraid it wasn't good enough coming from me. Maybe I was afraid they wouldn't accept it. Maybe I was just like my dad. I loved them all very much I just didn't know how to say it. My daughters and I have a little message. I learned it in the Bandidos. It's a coded message. I say it to my daughters all the time. It's the numbers 831. The meaning behind it is eight letters, three words, one meaning: I love you. So I usually would write this in the cards I'd give my daughters. I would also use it whenever I would text them.

Time takes its toll on everybody. Everyone has their breaking points. Diane was no different. I never loved any woman the way I loved her. She was everything I ever wanted in a woman. She was faithful. Instilled in her by her dear mother. I mean, this woman was faithful. A firecracker temper sometimes but a heart of gold. I knew from the beginning by her actions that she was a true faithful woman. Something I had never seen in a woman before. I appreciated her values but took them for granted.

My angry outburst had an impact on every one of my family members. My TBI had caused my mood disorder and I was out of control. Being the man I was, I never wanted to accept the fact that I needed help. The Veterans Administration was there all I had to do was go with my DD-214 and I would receive the needed help. I am a stubborn man and would not do it. I thought I was being strong by not addressing my problem. I continued my way of living. Lost without G-d, I had gone back on my word. Back when I was nineteen years old in basic training when I accepted Jesus Christ as my Lord and Savior. He never left me. I left him, I had turned my back on G-d almighty the one who had always seen me through everything. I was weak. I was a weak man. No different than most who live their lives as if they will never die.

I was arrogant. I would tell Diane I didn't need her. Deep inside, I knew I did. As men, we are conditioned to be strong. To not show emotion. To stand up and act as if we have it all together. I was living a lie. I didn't have it all together. The most beautiful woman I had ever met was mine in marriage. A blessing from G-d and I didn't even appreciate that G-d had answered my prayer when I asked him for a faithful wife. He gave her to me and I didn't even care. My pride kept me from actually thanking G-d for his many blessings in my life. For him saving my life many times. By encamping his angels around me. Giving me the protection.

I belonged to him. And once you belong to him, you are always his. What a great love G-d shows us. That no matter how we are he still loves us. We get angry with him and he still loves us. Sometimes, it's hard to fathom. How we as people will give up on others when G-d would never give up on us. We praise G-d and curse our fellow man. I pray that G-d teaches me his way. So I can be a better husband, father, and friend.

This journey that we have here on earth. Our purpose is to love G-d and love one another. Love one another the way he loves us.

Chapter 20

I had now been in the club for over five years. I had also transferred to the San Antonio chapter from the Hill Country chapter. I was always gone. On the road with the club and at a party with my brothers. Run after run, meeting after meeting. We had a meeting every Thursday. Fifty-two weeks a year. It was part of the club. I never attended church. But I attended every meeting as required. Ironically, many brothers referred to our meetings as church. I never took it as a mockery toward G-d. It was referred to by that name because it was weekly. At least that's how I saw it. Nevertheless, I didn't give G-d any of my time in real church, as I did to the weekly meetings I always attended. I was too consumed with myself and being part of the Bandidos MC. I wanted to make it a point of trying to be the best Bandido brother I could be. By making all the runs, parties, and meetings, I thought that it showed how dedicated I was to the club. I never was good at anything, but I was good at being a Bandido. At least I thought that I was.

From my probationary period to right after, I always had an officer position in the chapter. I was the secretary treasurer. In the ten years I spent as a member of the club, I held the position of road captain, secretary and treasurer, and the vice president. Being the secretary was a very important position. A position that worked close with the president. If anything was going on in the chapter, the secretary was always aware of it and always kept his president in the loop. The club was structured with officers and soldiers. The president, vice president, secretary which was almost always the treasurer also. Two sergeant at arms and a road captain. If you didn't hold an officer position, then you were a soldier. The vice president assumed the president's duty if the president wasn't there or he sometime would represent the president out of town on some kind of club business. Like I said, no matter what it was, the secretary was involved in all chapter business.

The sergeant at arms' job was first to protect the president. He also carried out internal discipline on members who violated the rules of the club. Some of the infractions a member might commit would be making the club look bad or disrespecting another brother. Getting caught lying was a big offense. Lying could even get you kicked out of the club. The same thing with shooting any kind of drugs. Shooting drugs is a low-life thing. People who are addicted would steal from their own mother. So if you were caught shooting drugs, you'd get a beat down and ran off. You would be put out of the club in bad standing. Out in bad standing was a term meaning like excommunicated, exiled, expel, banish, expatriate. You were never to show your face around the club or the motorcycle scene ever again. Most of the time if you were ran off, the chapter you belonged to would take your motorcycle.

Whichever infraction a member might commit if a green light was given by your president. (green light meaning permission or a go ahead), you might receive a black eye or get socked in the jaw by the sergeant at arms. One good sock usually made you get the message. Business is business. You got socked in the mouth and carried on. It was just taking care of club business. Nothing more and nothing less.

There was no animosity on the part of the sergeant at arms. He was just doing his job. As a member being disciplined, you had better not hold any animosity either or you'd be dealt with again. Maybe more severely next time. Everyone understood. There were some members who sometimes didn't get it. They would be beaten up good and ran off.

Members wore patches on their vests. Some indicating things that you understood by what it said. Phrases like Expect No Mercy. Which is in fact from a Bible scripture in the book of James 2: 13, "For he shall have judgment without mercy." Another patch that was worn was also from the Bible, but it was reversed. It read, "I am my brother's keeper." Genesis 4:9 says, "And the Lord said unto Cain,

Where is Abel thy brother? And he said, I know not: Am I my brother's keeper?" Someone who created this patch had to have knowledge of the scriptures. I recognized it right away. So I believe that there were others in the club like me who had a rooted foundation in the word of G-d. Why else would these patches come to be?

There were many other patches worn by various members. I noticed those two when I first became a member. Almost as if G-d were speaking to me. The Holy Spirit would always remind me of who I was. Of whose blood I was bought with. A price was paid for me along with the rest of mankind. My heavenly father loved me even though I was not serving him. We as fathers love our children because the same spirit that lives in us is the same as G-d's spirit. Only we are not capable of the love he has for us. His is beyond comprehension.

G-d has given us free will. To do as we wish. To live our lives as we want. Even though he doesn't want us to fall, he lets us so we can understand that being in his grace is where we belong.

Chapter 21

T he year was 2009. I had never really realized it, but my traumatic brain injury that happened while I was in the US Army had a big impact in my daily living. I continually had severe mood swings. I was very angry all the time. It seemed normal to me because I had been living this way for as long as I can remember. I was very mean to all my loved ones. My girls and Diane were the ones I would vent on. Believe me when I say I had no idea how bad my mood swings were. I feel really bad the way I treated my family. Sometimes the ones closest to us are who we take things out on.

Sometimes, being sorry just is not enough. People can only take so much. Diane and I seemed to argue all the time. We didn't seem to get along at all. I would get drunk all the time. I sat around the local bars. Some were close and some were not so close. I'd try to ease my guilt. I had always loved my family with all my heart like the next guy. I couldn't understand why I couldn't control my anger. It didn't matter. I thought everything would blow over. Most woman would have bailed out of a marriage like that in a heartbeat. I'm glad Diane wasn't like most women.

I remember Diane and I were arguing. It was a bad argument. Never physical but always yelling back and forth. It was hard to be around each other. It came to pass when she told me, "I wish you would just get out of here and never come back."

For some stupid reason, I told her, "Is that what you really want?"

She said yes. I know it was out of anger now, but at the moment, I didn't care. I didn't stop and think. My actions were that of impulse. I felt like all right I'm out of here. I packed my clothes and left. I grabbed a couch here and there at different houses for a few weeks until I could find a place to rent. I did rent a couple of rooms after too long. Both rooms were in Converse, Texas.

I never called Diane trying to reconcile with her. I thought she can call me. She was the one who said she wanted me to leave so why should I come crawling back to her. I was a fool; deep in my heart I loved her and missed her dearly. Men always have to show that we are strong. We can't for a moment let anyone think that we are weak.

My dear Pop used to tell me that a Salas doesn't show his weakness. If you have to cry, Steven, don't let anyone see you. So I cried alone sometimes. Sometimes I cried inside. I missed her every day. I filed for divorce after about a month of not hearing from her. I was convinced that she didn't love me anymore. I was convinced that I was born to lose. I would never have a life that I wanted to enjoy. I could hear my mother's words that she used to say to me when I was a little boy. Like it was yesterday. Her telling me that I was good for nothing. That I would never amount to anything. That I was just like my dad. She was right. Look at my life. I was all alone. My daughters were all grown and had been busy with their own lives. I'd get an occasional call from one of them now and then. I would put on the act that I was doing great even though I was dying inside. I had to remain strong for them at least. In event that one of my daughters had a crisis in their life. I had always been there for all my daughters. It wouldn't be any different now.

I couldn't show my weakness. My dad had made it clear. So I couldn't let him down. The phone calls with any of my daughters were always short. Shot but good. I used to love hearing from all of them. It always made my day whenever any of my daughters called me.

I eventually found a place to rent in Lake McQueeney, Texas. It isn't far from San Antonio. Maybe twenty miles or so. It's kind of an unusual place. On the lake, wealthy people build beautiful houses to get away from the city. They go there and drink their wine and enjoy water skiing, jet skis, and whatever else they want to. Ironically, my sister-in-law Denise and her husband, Dylan, have a beautiful house on the lake.

They didn't build it until some years later. Diane's other sister, Pam, and her husband had one before I met Diane, but they sold theirs before Diane and I got together.

Then there is another part of Lake McQueeney where the regular working class live. That's where I was living. The small house was on FM 725. It was a little one-bedroom with a small kitchen and living room together. It was perfect for me. It was right around the corner from a watering hole I liked to frequent. Night after night, I would drink myself drunk in Family Tradition on FM 78 right outside Seguin, Texas.

On the weekends mostly, but sometimes during the week, you could hear the roar of Harleys going up and down FM 725, the road right in front of my house. I fit in perfectly, being that I was an Outlaw biker. Occasionally, I would be pulling out and recognize an independent biker or a club member from a AMA club. I catch up to them and we'd end up in a corner of Family Tradition bar. Drinking cold Lone Star Beer and some whiskey from a bottle that someone brought inside with them.

I became part of the furniture if you will. That's how much I was there. Everybody knew me. It's funny how everyone wanted to be your friend as a Bandido. I can't say the same to this day. Most have long forgotten about me. My dad used to always tell me, "You really know who your friends are if you're dying or you are in the hospital or in jail." Yeah, my good Ol Pops. He sure was a wise man. He sure was right about that one. I've been long forgotten about.

A friend of mine that owned Family Tradition makes a point to contact me to this day still. Allen will text me usually on Veterans Day. He will simply put, "Hope you are doing well, Red." I always reply and say, "Thanks for thinking about me, amigo." You know it's good to get a surprise text from someone that you never see. That tells you that they are thinking of you. Those are the real friends.

It took some time for the divorce to finalize. I had retired from the City of San Antonio municipal government in 2008. I had a tow truck business and was running it. I remember thinking what will I do if I run into Diane. My heart would drop I'm sure. I missed her every day. Worse yet, what if I ran into her and she was with another man. I was a prisoner of my own mind. There was no escaping it. I never once thought about getting on my knees and asking my G-d to restore my marriage. I was too proud to do that. What an idiot I was.

Our divorce was finalized and that was it. I was supposed to be happy, right? Isn't that what a divorce is supposed to do? Make everyone happy once you're away from that other person.

I was miserable. Day after day, month after month, I never heard from Diane once. I never ran into her. I'd try to drink her off my mind, but it never worked. It just made me think of her more. Like an old country Western song lyrics, I'd drink her off my mind somehow.

I would end up in the little house I rented alone. Passed out in my clothes, boots, and all. I'd wake up and undress myself. Hoping I wouldn't get a tow call. I was hung over and didn't care about anything at that given moment. I just wanted to stay in bed all day.

I knew a guy named Arthur. He was a member of an AMA club. His wife was a schoolteacher at the elementary school down the street from where I lived. So Arthur was always around Lake McQueeney. Arthur was between jobs. He was a big muscular black guy. He had been working in the oil field. The oil field is hard work. It would get you into shape and it showed on Arthur.

We'd sit in the bar and drink beer. Arthur would drag his cigarette between swigs of his long neck. He was very soft spoken. He wasn't loud and boisterous. We'd talk about runs or benefits that were coming up in the areas surrounding where we lived. Drinking beer and listening to classic country music. Country music had to always go along with my beer.

Conversations after conversations led us to talking about my towing business one afternoon. I asked him if he'd be interested in driving the tow truck for me. He agreed. You see, I have a real good friend Jesse (Chuy) Arceo who owned a towing business in San Antonio. He taught me the ropes of the towing business. My business was doing good. It was another blessing from G-d. Chuy being such a good friend. He is always there for me to this day. He's the same kind of friend as Andrew. Both of these guys have been the kind of family brothers I never had. Andrew is a used-car salesman.

I met him through church. He has one of the biggest hearts. Chuy is the same way. Both of these friends have always been there for me no matter what. I know G-d put both of them in my path. I'm grateful to have both of them as friends. No matter what, if they can help me, they will. G-d bless them. I'm blessed to have them as close friends more like brothers.

Arthur agreed to run the tow truck from 6 p.m. to 6 a.m. and I would run it from 6 a.m. to 6 p.m. It helped me a lot because sometimes I could do anything. Anxiety, depression, mood swings, and a sleeping disorder kept me living an abnormal life.

I started to sink into a deep depression due to my TBI. That and along with trying to cope with losing the woman that I loved with all my heart. It came to pass where I didn't want to do anything, I would sit in my little house that I rented and shut the world off. Friends would call and stop by. I wouldn't answer the door to any of them. I wouldn't take their calls either. I just wanted to be by myself.

I asked for a leave of absence from the Bandidos. I was given six months of medical leave. Life had become too much to bear.

I went to Audie Murphy VA Hospital in San Antonio. I went in and explained to the ER that I had terrible mood swings. The nurse didn't seem to care. It was probably just me imagining it. I flew into a rage and they said if they would give me something that was going to help me with my problems. The nurse gave me an injection.

A male hospital worker came with a wheelchair and told me to sit down and relax. I took the seat as my mind began to drift. I saw the worker and the nurse starting to remove my boots and then they helped me remove my clothes. All while I didn't seem to care. My mind was drifting further and further. It reminded me of that song by Pink Floyd, "Comfortably Numb": Okay, okay, okay, just a little pin prick, there'll be no more, ahhhhhhhhhh, but you will feel a little sick.

They dressed me in hospital pajamas. I looked around, semi-disoriented wondering why all this was happening. The nurse said to me, "Mr. Salas, we are glad that you came to the VA hospital. We are going to help you. At least you didn't go to a civilian hospital. Your outburst would have caused you to go to jail. They wouldn't understand what's wrong with you. They really wouldn't have understood what was wrong with you in jail. I've reviewed your medical records and I see you had a traumatic brain injury while on active duty. We're going to get you help."

I woke up in the psychiatric ward of the VA hospital. I was very groggy; another vet said, "Man, you have been sleeping for two days." I didn't know what day it was and it took me time to think of what day I brought myself to the hospital.

Around the room, there were vets at different tables. Some playing chess, some watching TV, and some just sitting alone. Two doors separated the hospital bay from the main floor of the hospital. The only way out was to be buzzed out both doors. I saw what I thought to be nurses or nurses' assistants walking around with clipboards; they followed each individual and monitored their behavior. They did this so when the psychiatrist would come in to see you. The doctor would be able to see what your behavior was like that day. The vet that talked to me when I first woke up said, "You had better take your medicine when they give it to you or you will be in here for a year."

"A year?" I said.

"Yeah, the psychiatrist determines when you can go."

About that time, dinner was served. On those soft plastic trays. I guess it's so you can't use them as a weapon to hurt yourself or others. I took my tray like the others did. I walked off into a corner table by myself. I raised the spoon to my mouth and took a bite. My hand holding my spoon began to tremble. Then I began to cry. Tears streamed down my face. What had happened to my life? My life was ruined. I lost my wife. I had no friends. Look at me, I was crying in the open. Forgetting what my dad had always told me. Don't let anyone see you cry. Don't show your weakness to anybody. I felt so alone.

Medication and checking my vital signs became routine. I complied with the instructions of the staff. They called for a smoke break. I didn't smoke, but I wanted to go outside. On the patio was a high fence with razor wire on the top. There were men here with worse problems then me. I guess they didn't want you leaving. They wanted to give you the help you needed even if you didn't understand it.

Certain things happen in a person's life that stay with you forever. I spent Christmas 2010 in the VA hospital. A nurse announced that the American Legion post out of Universal City Texas was coming in to the ward to give us Christmas dinner. These kind souls that were full of compassion. The ladies filed in with everything you could think of. Turkey, ham, dressing, mashed potatoes, and different flavor pies. They gave each of us five dollar spending money for the vending machines. It really touched my heart. That strangers would go through all of this for all of us. I thought there still are good people left in this world.

The psychiatrist felt that I had made progress and that my current medication was helping me. After dozens of appointments with a neurologist, the Poly-Trauma unit at Audie Murphy VA hospital, a hearing specialist and of course the psychiatrist. I was diagnosed with traumatic brain injury, resulting in PTSD, cognitive disorder due to status post-traumatic brain injury with post-concussion syndrome, mood disorder with a bilateral hearing loss. I had a moderate hearing loss, partial loss of smell and taste due to the TBI. I was fitted for hearing aids a few months later. People have always said I always talked real loud. Diane use to say it constantly. It was because I had a hearing loss from being struck in the head with that chain.

I was released after two weeks. Within a few days of going back to my little house in Lake McQueeney, I received a call from the mental health clinic. I was assigned an RN (nurse); his name was Don. A devise was installed in my house that was plugged into my phone line. Every evening it would ring and ask me questions concerning my mental health. Do you feel like hurting anyone? Do you feel like hurting yourself? It got to be a pain in the neck. I was assigned a regular psychiatrist and a social worker, Karen. Both Don and Karen were great and very understanding. They were genuine and I knew they cared. I was always able to tell Karen all the things I could never tell anyone else.

Chapter 23

Not everything can be fixed with medication. Counseling and therapy play a big part as well. One night, I got it in me to go riding by myself. I rode down FM 78 in the direction of San Antonio. Out of Lake McQueeney, through Marion, then Santa Clara in a blink of an eye, Cibolo, and arriving in Schertz. The big World War II tank came into view that sits in front of the property. The VFW post parking lot is where I turned into. Kickstand down and putting my helmet on my mirror, I walked inside. I ordered my regular Lone Star Light and made my way across the smoke-filled room. Bikers were at most of the tables while your local alcoholics occupied every bar stool at the bar. Billowing smoke from patrons with paper currency in front of them made it easy for the bartender to retrieve payment for the next drink. The bartender would slap down liquor they ordered in a jiffy as the customer gestured them to keep the change for the tip jar. Throwing it into the nearest of the jars spread out in their locations around the bar while en route to the next person.

I recognized someone in the distance. It was Cody, the president of a motorcycle club that was part of the AMA in San Antonio. Cody was a tall black guy. Besides Arthur, black bikers were few and in between. Cody was a good friend of mine, so I pulled up a chair as he extended his hand in a slapping motion to meet my hand with a slap me five that ended with a firm handshake.

"How's it going, Red?" he asked.

"Oh good," I lied. I told him I was in the VA hospital for a couple of weeks.

"No kidding," he replied then taking a guzzle of his beer. "Everything okay?"

I said yeah, trying to make a joke of it. "They were examining my head."

He started laughing. I put it past him. He believed me, I thought. Other bikers gathered, pulling up seats, conversing with me and Cody. The beer was flowing and shots were being ordered. I was downing whiskey and beer all through the night. Whenever I was drinking, I was cutting up and having a good time. When all of a sudden, my mind would drift. She'd come to my mind again. Diane, the woman I loved so dearly.

I got up and walked out the bar exit. Nobody was noticing that I was walking out. Everyone was still laughing and having a good time. The alcohol had affected everyone and nobody was paying attention to me. I walked out, staggering, bumping into the walls as I made my way through the double glass doors into the dark and staring up at the bright parking lot light that was buzzing with moths and gnats. I looked down and spit. I found a dark area of the parking lot where I could relieve myself. After finishing, I walked aimlessly around, thinking of Diane. The whiskey had taken full effect on my brain. I was severely intoxicated.

With the time that had passed, Diane had changed her phone number. Of course, she didn't give it to me.

I was so drunk when a number just came to me. I mumbled it to myself. Talking like there was someone with me, but I was just drunk. I dialed it and it began to ring. The familiar voice answered, "Hello?"

I said in an inebriated voice, "Danica, is your mom there?"

She snapped at me, saying, "She doesn't want to talk to you," and hung up on me.

At that moment, I had finally swallowed my pride along with a bunch of beer and whiskey. I staggered to my Electra Glide. I put on my helmet and hit the electric start. I wrapped my header out a couple of times for no reason other than being drunk. I raised my kickstand, and into the night I went. Back the same route in which I traveled earlier that evening. My mind was blank as I watched for squad cars in my rearview mirror, switching back to the front quickly to scan the oncoming traffic in the event of a cop coming in the other direction.

Making it home, rounding the corner of FM 725, I gazed through blurred vision at the dark Shell gas station deserted because it had closed hours before I came home. Under the train bridge with the sound of the heavy weight from the train echoing as it rolled overhead. Finally turning in my driveway, parking and fumbling to get my key in the doorknob.

Walking through my bedroom door, I turned on the television. I used it to keep me company and help me sleep. Doing my best to undress myself then plopping into bed. What seemed like a few minutes, I woke to the sunlight coming through the venetian blinds. Looking up, I saw some infomercial with the guy saying how great the product was that he was selling. While walking to my bathroom as the guy on TV said, "But wait if you call right now," as I closed the bathroom door out of habit behind me. It was early in the morning on Saturday.

I dressed myself walked out the door and headed to another of my favorite watering holes. The Deer Crossing Saloon in Selma, Texas. The proprietor Ray was a real good friend of mine. He also rode a Harley Davidson. His saloon was frequented by bikers, cowboys rednecks, and quite a few schoolteachers. All different walks of life hung out in there. Everyone always got along with the others.

It couldn't have been but about 8 a.m. I always rose early from sleep for as far back as I can remember. Now it was early, but there were others like me that could drink in the morning like having a cup of coffee. So sometimes, we would meet for morning Bloody Mary's. Well, I pulled into the asphalted parking lot off of FM 1518 and found a parking space. From a distance, I could see others there hanging out sipping on their tomato juice concoctions.

I got a drink and greeted all who were present. It must have been about thirty minutes of me being there and my cell phone rang. I didn't recognize the number. Every now and then, something tells me to answer those numbers that I don't know. So I answered. On the other line, I heard a soft woman's voice. She said, "What are you doing?"

I immediately said, "Who is this?"

Then with a southern Texas drawl, she said, "Diane, who do you think?"

I got the reply that any man would get for not recognizing the only woman that should be calling you.

I must have been hungover so bad that I didn't realize it was her. The woman that still had my heart. G-d had her call me. A big smile came across my face. I said, "Oh, how are you? How have you been?"

Diane said, "I'm okay. What did you want? Danica said you called last night."

I said, "Yes, I'm sorry, I was whiskey drunk. Well, it was nothing. I was just real drunk last night." I paused and then said it again, "I got real drunk last night and was missing you."

Diane said in a somber way, "You missed me?"

I said, "I miss you every day."

Humbly, she said, "I miss you too, Steven."

It made me feel good inside. I hadn't felt this good in a very long time. Thank you G-d, it means so much to me. I spoke to him in my mind. Your blessings once again that I don't deserve.

I wanted to cut it short not to overdo it. You know I had not spoken to her in over a year at least. So I calmly said, "It was good hearing your voice."

She said, "It was good hearing yours too, Steven."

"Well, Diane, I guess I'll let you go."

In that moment, I had an epiphany. I blurted out, "I still love you and I'm just a stubborn man."

Again, in a somber voice, she said, "I still love you too."

I can't express in words just how good that made me feel. I felt like someone who had just won the Texas Lottery. I said again, "Okay, I'll let you go. Can I call you sometime?"

Diane said, "Do you want to have lunch?" Ignoring my question.

It didn't take me a moment to think. I said, "Sure, when?"

Then in her playful voice that I knew so well, she said, "I don't know, we'll talk again."

I said, "Sure, okay."

That same voice was the voice I remember when I first dated her. She was a moral woman with a good family.

Her parents and siblings were all decent good people. The kind you just don't see any more. All of the family were always good to me. Never judging me even though I was in an Outlaw Motorcycle Club. The Bandido reputation was well-known, but they didn't judge a book by the cover. It made me feel good. Knowing that they accepted me as I was. The way my dad would make me feel.

Now they were traditional Texans. Diane's dad was a tall slender man with grey hair and a full grey beard. He was of English descent and I remember their last name ringing a bell. It was similar to the poem by Alfred Tennyson, "The Charge of the Light Brigade."

> Half a league, half a league,
> Half a league onward,
> All in the valley of Death
> Rode the six hundred.
> "Forward, the Light Brigade!
> Charge for the guns!" he said.
> Into the valley of Death
> Rode the six hundred.
> "Forward, the Light Brigade!"
> Was there a man dismayed?
>
> Not though the soldier knew
> Someone had blundered.
> Theirs not to make reply,
> Theirs not to reason why,
> Theirs but to do and die.
> Into the valley of Death
> Rode the six hundred.
>
> Cannons to right of them,
> Cannons to left of them,
> Cannons in front of them
> Volleyed and thundered;
> Stormed at with shot and shell,
> Boldly they rode and well,

Into the jaws of Death,
Into the mouth of hell
Rode the six hundred.

Flashed all their sabres bare,
Flashed as they turned in air
Sabring the gunners there,
Charging an army, while
All the world wondered.
Plunged in the battery-smoke
Right through the line they broke;
Cossack and Russian
Reeled from the sabre stroke
Shattered and sundered.
Then they rode back, but not
Not the six hundred.

Cannons to right of them,
Cannons to left of them,
Cannons behind them
Volleyed and thundered;
Stormed at with shot and shell,
While horse and hero fell.

They that had fought so well
Came through the jaws of Death,
Back from the mouth of hell,
All that was left of them,
Left of six hundred.

When can their glory fade?
O the wild charge they made!
All the world wondered.
Honour the charge they made!
Honour the Light Brigade,
Noble six hundred!

Oddly enough, when I first heard my wife's maiden name, that poem was the first thing that came to my mind. Some of you may know this poem and some may not. Some of you could care less.

Now before my TBI, I never was much good in school. I never made grades above Cs. It seems after my TBI, my long-term memory increased big time. Whenever I'm doing things, something will fly into my head like with their last name and "The Charge of the Light Brigade."

Diane's dad and me got along real well He was a great hunter. His trophy room was full of all kinds of game animals. White-tail deer, elk, caribou, black bear, moose lined the walls of their den. He also was an angler. He landed a huge blue marlin that he also had on his wall. So we would have long conversations about the outdoor. He is great father-in-law. The kind everyone wants. My mother-in-law was a small lady. Small but strong. Strong in the way as a matriarch of their family. A tough little cookie. She as well always received me with warm hospitality. I think I missed their family hospitality as much as I missed Diane during the divorce. My in-laws, Pam, Jr. and Denise, were all the same. Good people all the way around. Diane was the baby of the family.

Diane and I eventfully started seeing each other again regularly. It made me feel some kind of ease. I felt as if for once, my life was getting back to normal again. With my continued mental health treatment and my medications, I started to be able to calm the unbridled wild horse demeanor that I had displayed for so many years. The inner demons that plagued my mind began to subside as well.

I loved her company and she loved mine. All our kids were grown now and they were working and attending to their own lives. It gave us more freedom from the responsibility that we had when we were raising all of them. Diane had always been there for my daughters and treated them like a real mother would. The kind I never knew and the kind their mother never wanted to be.

Chapter 24

H olidays are always special around Diane's family. I had two sisters-in-law and a brother-in-law. This wholesome family always made me feel part of their family. Growing up was nothing like this. Never in my life do I recall holidays the same as my time with Diane's family

Beautiful tables laid out of delicious food. Turkey, ham, dressing, and all kinds of sides. Beautiful decor throughout the house matching the theme of the holiday being celebrated. The kind of table I used to dream of as a boy. This is really what families do. This is how they really act. They gather with one another and enjoy each other's company all while having dinner.

My mother-in-law is one heck of a cook. Everything from scratch. I'll never know how my father-in-law stayed so thin. If Diane's mother cooked for me every day, I would be as big as a house. Pam, Denise, Diane, and Dylan's sister always made the best of food. Everyone brought covered dishes. I think cooking good runs in their family.

My sister-in-law Denise and her husband Dylan always hosted the holiday in their beautiful home. Never making me feel uncomfortable. I'm sleeved all the way on both arms. I have a tattoo across my throat, on my back, my stomach, and on my hands. I used to have superlong hair down to the middle of my back. I always wore a goatee. My auburn hair and red beard were my trademark sort a speak. So these get-togethers were always good because I fit in even if I didn't look the part. Fond memories I will always have.

Diane and I were a couple again. G-d had shown mercy on me and restored my relationship with her. She wasn't my wife, but I still considered her to be. My life had been a train wreck for the longest time, but G-d started putting it back together. I never wanted to be without Diane again. She was an answered prayer after my first wife left me with my girls for another man. Diane was the woman of my dreams. She was raised right and was a faithful woman and wife to me. What more could a man want or hope for?

The time came when there was a get-together with Diane's family. She said, "You are going to go with me, right?"

I said, "I don't know."

You see, I had not been around her family in the time that we were divorced. I said, "I mean all that we have been through." I'm sure nobody is going to be happy to see me.

Diane said, "Don't be ridiculous, nobody is mad at you."

I should have known better. I knew how the whole family was and how I had always been treated. I reluctantly went with her.

We approached the front gate of the wealthy subdivision where Denise and Dylan lived. I began to get nervous and felt uncomfortable as we drove away from the guard shack and through the fancy front gates of the luxurious private neighborhood. Down the streets we drove, passing one expensive beautiful house after another. Finally making the final left turn to the cul-de-sac to the front of the House. I parked our vehicle while looking at the decorations on the facade that Denise always took pride in having. The manicured lawn with a perfect landscape. Expensive luxury vehicles in the driveway showed how successful of a businessman Dylan was.

Diane grabbed a few items from the back seat as I hesitated to get out. I fumbled with my phone while making an excuse.

"Ah, I'll be right there, Diane. I have to make a call."

It was a lie that I conjured up to not have to go in. Minutes passed by and Diane soon appeared in the doorway. She looked puzzled at why I had not come in the house yet. She gestured with her hands like "What's up?" and then motioned with a wave for me to come in. Looking straight at her, I froze and totally ignored her repeated request to exit the car and come inside. She started to approach the car while her steps were firm and her expression was one of aggravation.

"What are you doing?" she asked.

I came clean. "I'm worried that everyone will not be happy to see me. I know your dad won't for sure."

Her dad was a stand-your-ground Texan. As most are. He wouldn't hesitate to defend his wife in a heartbeat. Even if it meant losing his own life to protect her. I can only imagine how he felt about the guy who divorced his daughter. The baby of their family.

I don't know about most but fathers who have daughters are not the kind to tangle with. I'm that way as most men are. I said, "You know with the divorce and all."

"Don't be ridiculous, Steven," she said abruptly. "I already said nobody is mad at you."

I said, "I'll just wait out here."

Diane stormed off and said okay.

If I know Diane and her mother, like I do. Diane went inside and said to her mother, "He won't come inside, Momma," in her voice with her drawl. I'm sure her mother said, "What?" Then she probably told Diane's dad, "You better go out there and let him know you are not mad." I'm assuming that's how it went.

I thought that because a moment later, her dad in fact did appear in the entrance of the house. He walked toward me. Nervous as heck, I didn't know what to expect. He offered me his hand and said, "Well, hey, Steve, how are you? How have you been?"

You should know I immediately accepted his hand and shook it firmly.

"Fine, sir," I replied.

He said, "Why don't you come in?"

I couldn't deny the personal invitation of the head of this family. That would have been an insult to a man who was always decent to me. I walked as we small-talked about something or another. Inside I was met by Denise's big smile and a hug. "Hi, Steve. It's nice to see you."

Next was Pam with her soft voice and her delightful smile. "Hello, Steven."

Diane's mother said, "Well, hello, Steve."

Dylan approached me and gave me a firm handshake while saying, "How's it going, big guy?"

It was the way they had always all been. I was very relaxed knowing her family still accepted me. The evening carried on with many different conversations. I was at ease, thanks to everyone around me. I walked through the large-scale house gazing out the window.

I watched the invisible wind blowing the fall leaves around by the glare of the street light. Another thing had been given back to me by G-d. The acceptance of a family. I felt so at home, so welcome, so much at peace. I said a silent prayer to G-d. I don't know why you love me the way you do, Lord. I turned my back on you. I walked away from your grace. I felt conviction and ashamed of myself. I had lost it all.

Just like Job. Only he was faithful, obedient, and loved G-d with all his heart. As Job sat there covered in sores, covered in ashes, Job's wife said to him, "Why don't you curse G-d and die?"

Job replied, "Thou he slay me yet will I praise him. Naked I came from my mother's womb and naked I will depart. The Lord gives and the Lord has taken away. May the name of the Lord be praised."

I remember having a scripture tattooed across my throat written in Hebrew from the book of Job 30:20 I cry out unto you G-d but you don't answer. With an exception of maybe two tattoos, all of my tattoos are scripture illustrations. I covered myself in them while fighting my sickness. Fighting my demons instead of letting G-d fight my battles. I put my faith in myself instead of in him. My life was nothing compared to G-d's servant, Job.

The night eventfully began to wind down with the family guests slipping away one after another. It was a pleasant evening. One that I hadn't experienced in a while. I felt good inside and out.

Chapter 25

J uly 2011, I came back off my medical leave of absence from the Bandidos. I attended my first meeting with the San Antonio Chapter. It had been out for six months. All the brothers were in the parking lot of Hooligan's Bar in Live Oak. I was greeted as I walked up to the crowd of standing brothers.

With big hugs and handshakes. Slaps on the back and greetings of "Hey, brother, how have you been?" Logan, Frank our president, Hank, Mark, Martin. My good buddy Raymond AKA my road dog. A term used for brothers who are always riding together. My good friend Jack and Joe were both in federal prison at the time. We held the meeting as we always did. chugging long-neck bottles of beer until Frank called for the meeting. Members began informing other brothers that might be in conversation or playing pool. Saying, "Hey, it's time, let's go." The meeting was called to order and the same things were discussed as usual. Club business, any upcoming runs. Any news about brothers sick, in the hospital, or jail. The meeting ending with anyone have anything? Giving each brother an opportunity to bring up anything they wanted to be addressed.

The night ended with my chapter closing down the bar. Unless you were a member who had to rise early for your job. Yes, jobs. I know some would have you think that Bandidos don't work. They do. Like I said earlier, they're regular men like everyone else. They love their families. They have mortgages, bills, and other living expenses like the rest of us. These guy were the friends that I cared about. I would have thought that they felt the same as I did. I'm sure that they did.

A lot had been pressing on my mind. I don't recall where I was or what I was up to. I just remember it coming to my mind to call Frank. The time I had off from the club. My time alone. My time in the VA hospital. Most of all G-d's conviction. All of these factors played a key part in me calling Frank one day. I pressed the keys on my keypad of my cell phone. The signal connected after a brief moment. It rang and rang some more. I didn't think he was going to answer.

Finally, I heard his voice come and say yeah.

"Hey, brother, it's me Red."

Always sounding serious to me, he said, "What's going on, Red?"

I said, "Well, I have something I want to tell you."

He said, "Well, what's up?"

I said, "I want to retire out of the club."

He was silent for a split second and said, "Why, what's up, brother."

I said, "Well, I've been in ten years and I just want to retire."

He tried to persuade me by saying, "You know once you decide there's no turning back. The San Antonio chapter had a rule if you transferred to another chapter from ours, you could not come back to the San Antonio Chapter."

I guess he was extending that rule to someone wanting to retire. I said, "I know, brother. I want to retire."

Frank said, "I'll let you think about it."

I said, "I don't need to think about it, I just want to retire."

He said, "I'll give you a month. Think about it for a month."

I said all right. We ended our conversation; the cell connection dropped. I put the phone back in my Wrangler denim shirt pocket.

I stood daydreaming about nothing for a moment. I came back to my senses. I rode off and made my way back to Lake McQueeney.

Now I had been living in the little rented house for maybe a year or so. In all that time, I was trying to buy a house. I didn't think I had a chance because from my divorce, my credit went from excellent to about the low five hundreds. I had a realtor searching the Guadalupe, Wilson, and Comal counties. I wanted to live away from everybody and everything. For the most part, I just wanted peace and quiet. I wanted to rest and stop running in the fast lane.

A month had passed and I called Frank again and told him I stilled wanted to retire. He said he respected my decision. He told me to turn in all my Bandido property to the secretary. Before we hung up, Frank said, "Take care, brother. Come by, don't be a stranger."

He was referring to come by a meeting, party, or a run sometime. I said, "All right, I'll try."

The call ended.

The property he was referring to was anything and everything that had the Fat Mexican, 1%ER, the name Bandidos MC, or anything else related to the club with any logo on it. This was a strict rule. A rule that you knew not to defy. The consequences and repercussion would be dire. I knew it and so did ever other past member and the current member. I was allowed to keep my motorcycle. When you come into the Bandidos, you willfully pledge your motorcycle for two years. You turn in your title. After two years elapse, you get the title back. I now would have the status of retired member Bandido Texas Red1%ER Charter member of the San Antonio chapter.

A few days later, I met with Hank to inventory all my stuff and turn it in. We said our goodbyes to each other. With that, I got in my truck and headed out of San Antonio. I jumped on Loop 1604 and headed towards IH-35 north. I was leaving behind my good friends. The ones I called my brothers. I felt bad inside. I had come to know these guys so good. Some of their kids even used to call me Uncle Red. I sighed and looked out the window. I looked at all the new construction along the access road. Restaurants were being built with signs proclaiming coming soon. Heavy equipment on pads of road base developing whatever was in the blueprints. New apartment communities for people wanting to escape the San Antonio inner city. My attention abruptly interrupted as my exit sign to the approaching IH-35 interchange came into view. Soon after, I eventfully ended up back in Lake McQueeney as always.

Chapter 26

I found me a house in Marion. It's a small town of about one thousand people in Guadalupe county. Marion was named in honor of Marion Dove, whose grandfather, Joshua W. Young, owned a plantation that the Galveston, Harrisburg, and San Antonio Railway passed through in 1877. It's a small diverse community of mostly German and Mexican people. There isn't much there as small as it is, but I liked it.

My credit score was bad and I knew it but the realtor said, hey, don't worry trying to make a sale. I did all the paperwork for my mortgage. I was shocked that my application came back approved. G-d once again saw me through another obstacle of this world. I was ecstatic. I started getting boxes and packing all my household items while the closing was taking its course.

The day had come when I received the keys to my new house in Marion. I had a few friends from the biker bar in Lake McQueeney that had volunteered to help me with my move. There was about six pickups in all. We moved everything in one shot. That is the best way to move if you are ever going to move. All the trucks follow in a makeshift convoy. When you get to where you are going. It might take forty-five minutes to unload all the pickups and carry all the contents inside. Each box is taken to its room as marked on the box. All that is left to do is unpack it all and arrange your house.

After we finished unloading, I went back to the rent house to clean it up to ensure I would get my security deposit back. I did in fact get the security deposit back. It came in handy for the water service deposit in Marion. That same evening, I returned to my new house. I began to unpack. It went late into the night. When I was pretty much finished, it actually looked and felt like a home again. I took a bite off my Little Caesar's pizza and a swig of my soda. Looking around the interior of the house I felt good. G-d had made the impossible possible. My credit score was horrible. The mortgage approval should have never happened. I recall the scripture from Matthew 19:26: Jesus looked at them and said, "With man this is impossible, but with G-d all things are possible." He truly did make it possible for me.

So in the following days and weeks to come, I did what any other person does when the buy a house. You make it look the way you want it to look.

The first thing I did was install my flag pole in the middle of the front yard. I raised Ol' Glory high and put her in her place. With a flood light shining on her for in the night. Her body rippling by the warm occasional Texas breeze. I was proud of my military service. I love America, and I love our flag, the true symbol of freedom.

I'm a man so I didn't have any flowers. I'd wait for Diane to take care of that. A woman's touch can always be recognized. They have a touch that can't be matched by a man. I tended to the yard. Cutting the crass and running the weed eater over the many spots that needed it. The grass had been cut regularly it appeared when I bought it. The trimming wasn't maintained, so I took care of it.

So G-d was working out all kinds of things in my life again. I didn't feel that I was doing what I should be doing to please him. I have never thought of myself as a good example of a Christian. I was humble in heart and always feared G-d but for me to set an example of what a Christian should be, let's just say, you didn't want to follow my lead. I'm not the worst or the best. I just keep on trying to be a good Christian. I mess up and ask for forgiveness. We are blessed to be loved by G-d. His mercy endures forever and ever. So when I fall short, I pray to him and ask his forgiveness. Thank G-d for his forgiveness. Where would any of us be? I know I for one would have been in hell a long time ago.

Chapter 27

Proverbs 18:22
 He who finds a wife finds a good thing, And
obtains favor from the LORD.

T hank G-d for second chances. Diane and I were in an exclusive relationship again. It was good to spend time with her. Nothing was going to get in my way of me loving her properly again. I've told her before many times that her presence is enough for me. I missed her so bad when we were apart. I think just knowing she is in my presence has reassured and reminded me the value of her. The value of her as a wife.

Diane had hung on as long as she could with her house payment. In the divorce, she was awarded our house. She tried to keep up with the payment; it proved to just too much for her. I couldn't help her, being that I had just got a new mortgage myself.

She was very depressed about losing her house. I felt bad and wished there was something I could do about it. Unfortunately, there wasn't anything I could do. She said she didn't know what she was going to do or where she would go. I told her what did she mean? She was the woman I loved. The woman that G-d brought back into my life for a second chance. She's a beautiful woman and could have easily met someone else and I would have been history.

So I told her, "You have a home with me. You can move in with me." She agreed it was time to let go of the house in Adkins. Let the bank have it. She eventually moved in and left that part of our life behind. Diane added her much needed touch to our home in Marion. You could tell a woman lived there. Western decor has always been Diane's favorite. I always liked it too.

I remember I used to have a tray table by the side of the bed before she moved in. She immediately said, "This is gone."

I said, "Hey, that's where I eat at. I need it there."

She said, "Not anymore, you don't you eat on the table like a normal human being."

I laughed it off and agreed. You know a good woman always makes a good home.

Proverbs 31:10 "An excellent wife who can find? She is far more precious than jewels."

Proverbs 18:22 "He who finds a wife finds a good thing and obtains favor from the lord."

Proverbs 12:4 "An excellent wife is the crown of her husband."

I don't recall when it was, but we were together doing something. I asked her out of the blue, "Diane, will you marry me again?"

She said, "Do you really want to be married to me again?"

I said, "Yes, I do. I want you to be my wife again."

She embraced me and said, "I never stopped loving you, Steven. I'd thought about you all the time. I'd hear songs on the country station and I'd have to change it because it made me think of you."

I held her tight and told her I was so glad she never stopped loving me. My whole life I just wanted to be loved and wanted it to be real.

Remembering back once again when I was a kid, I remember my dad and I were disagreeing on something. My dad told me, "I know why you're so angry, Steven. You so angry because all you want is for your mother to love you."

My eyes started tearing. I held it in like he taught me. I didn't answer him. I just walked off. As I walked away, he said, "I will always love you, son." He was right. I just wanted her to accept me. I really needed to let that go and heal. Even though she had passed away twenty years ago, I still hung on to my anger toward her. I didn't lose. I've had a very blessed life. I've had a prosperous life.

The day came, May 25, 2013, it was the day we would wed again. In our living room, we stood together. A friend of mine, Robert, is an ordained minister. Robert and I are members of the Disabled American Veterans, Douglas Herrle Chapter # 61. in Seguin. Robert was the chaplain there. That's how I got to know him.

We exchanged our vows in front of him and before G-d. The twins, Danica and Danielle, were our witnesses. We placed our wedding rings on each other and sealed it with a kiss. Robert congratulated us. We both thanked him and he departed shortly after.

My life had seemed to all fall back in place again. The blessings of G-d in my life. He restored many things for me in my life. Most importantly, Diane was in my life once again. She was my wife again.

Everyday life in Marion is simple. There a only a few businesses. Three or four restaurants, tire shop, a couple of gas stations, feed store, and an old-time hardware store. The kind of hardware store from my childhood. It has everything. I frequent it often because of that alone. I always joke and say at six p.m., they roll up the sidewalks in Marion. It's very quiet and peaceful. Crickets and the sound of the passing train is all that you will hear. I'm sure it's the same route that was there when Marion was established.

Going through town, I wave to folks, they wave back. It's a Texas thing. Everyone always waves. Even if they don't know you. In this town, they have come to know me well.

I stop by one of the convenience stores for a cold drink and a break from the sweltering Texas heat. I converse with the proprietor briefly. I walk next door to the tire shop and say what's up to the shop owner. I visit with an elderly black man that is regular visitor to the tire shop. He sits around and chews the fat with other locals or patrons that are waiting for their tire work to be completed. Soon, I move on. I head home or ride out to one of the ranches I hunt on. I've become an avid hunter, fur trapper, angler, and snake wrangler. It's what I occupy my time with mostly. I also a ham radio operator.

Marion has the Country Church. Diane and I attend church there. Pastor Butch Ikles officiates. He is a great pastor. A true man of G-d. He has definitely been called by G-d. I always get spiritually fed there. The country church does so much for the community. The way a church should be. Diane and I both like it very much.

Chapter 28

The year was 2015. By now, I was established and a regular member of the Marion general community. Most people knew who I was. The majority of business owners knew me because I would patronize their business on a regular basis. I had even served on the Marion Planning and Zoning Commission. What I'm sure most didn't know was, I was a former/retired member of the Bandidos MC and I'm sure some never even heard of the Bandidos MC until May of 2015.

I was tired and decided to take a nap. It was a nice May afternoon. Not cool and not blazing hot. Just right, good napping weather. I slept for a good while. When I woke, Diane was folding laundry. She said, "Someone keeps calling you." She doesn't care much about a cell phone. She isn't your norm when it comes to them. So any noise she hears, she says someone was calling me. Whether it's a notification from a text, e-mail, Facebook, or whatever. To her, your phone was ringing. Still rubbing my eyes, I tried to focus on phone lying on the nightstand. I finally recognized it and picked it up. There must have been at least thirty-five text messages. I was blown away how could so many text messages come through in the short period that I slept. I opened them one by one.

Each basically saying the same thing. "Are you okay? Were you there? Call me back, please let me know you're okay." Friends from every place near and far. Out-of-state friends and relatives frantic to get an answer from me. I called someone back and said, "What the heck is going on?"

"Haven't you seen TV?"

"No, what's up?"

"The Bandidos and the Cossacks had a big shootout in Waco, Texas, at Twin Peaks Restaurant. Nine people are dead and over twenty injured."

"Oh my G-d." My mind raced as I ignored more details the person was giving. My thoughts were Raymond, Jack Logan, and many more of my brothers. I acknowledged the caller even though I hadn't heard the rest of what all they were saying to me. All I was thinking about was my brothers.

I began calling them as fast as I could dial the numbers. I still had my old phone list from long ago. I called Jack and it went to voice mail. I called again same thing, then Logan. Logan had changed his cell number so I went to the next. Raymond my road dog. No answer. I called his house and his wife said he wasn't there. Oh G-d, please let them be safe in Jesus's name. I called Bandido Harvey, another good brother of mine who was very organized and intelligent. Harvey had been in the Bandidos forty-three years. I dialed and waited for the connection and then the ring. Within a few minutes, Harvey answered as he always did with a loud "What?" Then he laughed as he always did.

I said, "Harvey, this is Red."

He said, "Red on the head (referring to me being a red head)"

I said, "Is everyone in our chapter all right? I heard nine are dead and over twenty wounded."

He said, "The accountability wasn't all spoken for. Most were okay and arrested." He'd find out more later. He said Raymond was okay. Jack and Logan were in jail. After getting brief details of what he knew, our call ended.

That night, it was all over every news channel. It even made international news. This was a very big news story. It was covered by every news station practically. The days and weeks to come would give more detail on what exactly transpired that afternoon. Within a week, I found out that everyone was being held on one million dollars bond. So much for the eighth amendment. Excessive bail shall not be required, nor excessive fines imposed, nor cruel and unusual punishments inflicted. If you were a Bandido, you were hated by the law enforcement. There was nothing you could do. You were considered criminals. Even though more police officers get arrested than

Bandidos all the time. It didn't matter. The club had a reputation for being ruthless. More of a stereotype in my opinion. They were still all my brothers.

I began to ask G-d in prayer to ensure the judges were honest and fair. Most hadn't done anything but be there. Some were eating burgers when everything broke out. Guilt by association. If you were there and you had a Fat Mexican on your back, you were guilty until proven innocent. Time would only tell how long they'd be behind bars. Even if they were released, they'd all be on nonassociation with the club. If they were caught around the club, their bond would be revoked and back to jail they'd go.

I finally got to talk to Jack once the bond were finally reduced about three weeks later if I recall right. I called him on the phone. He said he was doing all right. I didn't ask him any details about the shootout. I was just glad I was able to speak to him. I was glad he was all right. I thanked the Lord for his protection of my brothers. None had been killed or wounded. It was just the beginning of a long litigation battle for all who were in Waco that day.

I stop and started to think. I thought about the mercy of G-d and how he knew this was in the future and removed me from being any part of it. I had been retired from the club for four years. I thanked him for his protection.

I reflected a time when we all road to a swap meet in DFW (Dallas, Fort Worth) at the old Billy Bobs dance hall. When we got there, another club was there, the Banshees, another 1 percenter club (Outlaw Motorcycle Club). There were plenty of them there. When they saw all the Bandidos, their number soon faded. Soon there were none there. Without incident, everyone checked out the deals at the swap meet. After it was over, some headed out for something to eat and some hit the bars. I stayed the night in a cheap hotel. You typical motel ran by a friendly Eastern Indian.

Everyone knew what had transpired in Waco. It was on the news for months. I still had contact with individuals I had met in the biker scene. A lot of them were friends I could call on to help me pray about stuff. My good prayer warriors that could always be depended on.

Andrew, the used-car dealer from San Antonio who I had known since the days at Pastor John Hagge's Cornerstone Church. There was my first Bandido president who left the club and gave his life to Christ. Irma Martinez who was always willing to pray. Along with Kate Garcia. Everyone said the same thing. They couldn't believe what had happened. Irma and Kate said they were glad none from San Antonio died or were hurt. Both said they would be praying for the brothers and their families. More than anything, all the people who contacted me said they were glad I was not part of it and nowhere near Waco. It made me feel good to know people cared about my well-being.

Since the time of the Waco incident, some other major arrests had come down. Some people involved in the murder of the guy who killed Bandido James. They already had one other guy in prison who pleaded guilty.

Then there was the murder of Anthony Benesh. Who was trying to start a chapter of the Hells Angels in Austin, Texas. He was shot and killed in front of his wife and kids. The three alleged perpetrators were all arrested for the Benesh murder. These guys too were guys I knew and were in the San Antonio Region Chapters. A whole lot was going to hit the fan. So many brothers were going to be facing serious charges. It seemed like all the different things came down at one time.

I looked back across my life from childhood to where I am now. I had a lot of things that looked like a bad life. Obstacles, disappointments, friends that let me down. People who I thought were friends who really were not. A mother that never loved me. Infidelity by my first wife. My dad passing away at fifty-seven years old. Fired from job after job. Never really being real good at anything. Brothers in my club dying. Brothers in the club going to prison. It was bad thing after bad thing in my life.

I've always have tried to be a good husband to Diane. A good father to all the kids. A friend that you could always depend on. Those things I've tried my best to be as good as I could be. I know I wasn't always the best to them. Like I said, I've tried my best not to let people down.

Yes, throughout my life, there had been many things around me that should have ended my life. With death or incarceration. But Jesus Christ is my Lord and Savior. My G-d knows my heart. You and I can never hide in our hearts anything from G-d. He is the merciful father. He has seen me through all the things of my life.

My life reminds me of the story that Jesus told, the story of the Prodigal Son.

There was a very rich man. This had two sons. The first son was a very hard worker. He always listened his father. He was very good and nice young man. But the man's second son was totally different from his oldest son. He was lazy. He did not work for his father or in his father's field. He was disobedient to his father. He wanted to lead an easy and free life.

One day, the man's youngest son said to his father, "Father, give me my share of property and money." This made the father feel very bad because he loved both of his sons very much. He divided his property and possessions and gave his younger son what was to be his. The younger son took his share of what his father gave him. Then he left home with his share of the money. He went to a distant land. There he made a lot of friends. Or what he thought were his friends. The same as today things don't change much. He spent his part of his inheritance on lavishly living and on his friends, foods and drinks. He had allot of bad habits. He wasted all the money his father had given him. Soon he was left with no money and was totally broke. All of his friends saw this. They all deserted him one by one. Just like the way my dad used to tell me. He'd say, "Steven, everyone wants to be your friend when you have money and beer. When you don't have more, you won't have any friends anymore either."

At that time, a great famine spread through the land were this young man was living. He could not get a job, he couldn't find any work to support himself anywhere. None of his so-called buddies offered to give him food, money, or a place to sleep. They all forgot about him now that he was broke. He was forced to take a disgusting job. A man gave him a job feeding his pigs. Sometimes, he even ate the food that was meant for the pigs. He was very sad about the way he was living. He had come from a wealthy family that had everything they needed. He soon came to his senses. He started to think about his father and his brother all the time. He thought, *In my father's house, even the ones that worked for him always had enough to eat and drink. They have good living conditions also and never worry where they will sleep. Here, I am struggling just to find something to eat and find a place to lay my head to sleep every night. I will go back to my father's house. I will beg him to hire me as one of his workers."*

So he got up and collected the little things he owned; the prodigal son left and started out for his father's house. All the time that he was gone, his father never stopped loving him or thinking of him. Just as G-d did in my life. The man would sit near his windows. He would always sit and look toward the road, hoping his young son would return home.

One day, the man saw his son coming from a distance. He ran out of his house overcome with emotion and down his road. He was overwhelmed with joy at the sight of his young son as he recognized him. He met the young son halfway down the road. His son knelt down before his father. He said, "Father, I am not fit to be called your son. Hire me as your workers."

His father lifted him to his feet. He hugged him. He held his son so tight. He turned to his workers. He said, "Bring the best robe. Put it on my son. Put a ring on his fingers and shoes on his feet. Kill the fatted calf. Prepare a giant feast. Let us all eat and celebrate. My son was lost. Now he is found."

The older son was coming from working in the field. He heard the sound of the music and celebrating coming from the house. He asked one of his workers what was going on. The worker told the older son, "Your brother came home. Your father is celebrating that he came home safe. A fatted calf has been killed to cook for a delicious feast and they are having a celebration."

The older son got very angry. He refused to even go into the house. His father came out and begged the older son to come in and celebrate with them. The older son said, "I have listened to you all these years. I have worked very hard for you all the time. But you never even gave me even a goat to enjoy with my friends. This son of yours who wasted all your money and property comes back and you kill a fatted calf for him!"

The father replied, "My dear son, you are always with me and I love you. All that I have and own is yours. But don't you see, your younger brother was dead. Now he is alive. He was lost. Now he is found. Therefore we should rejoice."

The older son eventully understood the love behind the words that the father had spoken. He forgot everything about his younger brother and forgave him. He decided to take part in the celebration. They all celebrated and were happy. Even though I wandered off from the grace of my savior, he waited for me to return home to him again. I wanted to live my life. I wanted to live the way I thought was living. G-d let me go. He said, "You are still my child and I still love you. Go find out for yourself."

I feel the same as the prodigal son. I always asked G-d to help me from the time I was a boy. All that I went through as a child. After accepting Jesus Christ as Lord and Savior, it wasn't good enough. I wanted to live the way I thought was living. I did everything against my heavenly father's wishes for me. Even though I didn't deserve his love, grace, and protection, he saw me through it all. My life could have been a lot different like many of my Bandido brothers. G-d had other plans for me. One day, I woke up sort of speaking. I said, "I'll go back home." I'll go back to where it all started when I met the Lord. I'll go back and ask G-d to forgive me. He restored so much in my life. I praise the mighty name of G-d. I was a prodigal son.

Because like the prodigal son, I returned.

About the Author

Steven (Red) Salas is today living in a small South Texas town outside of San Antonio. He lives with his wife, Diane, and granddaughter, Dahla, one of their eight grandchildren.

He spends most of his time hunting, fishing, fur trapping, and snake wrangling. He is an avid outdoorsman. He's well-known in his community and uses to serve on the planning and zoning commission. He and his wife are members of the Country Church.

It's not uncommon to see Red driving daily through town in his camouflage 4×4 hunting SUV. After scouting some local ranches in the area, he stops into a few of the local businesses to visit with the proprietors and local residents.

He is a ham radio operator. He's part of the Amateur Radio Emergency Services and Skywarn in his county. He provides snake removal free of charge for the residents of his town and for the city and county police. He specializes in pit viper removal

He's a life member of the Disabled American Veterans the Doug Herrle Chapter 61 of Seguin, Texas, a life member of the Texas Trappers and Fur Hunters Association, and life member of the NRA.

If you happen to run into him on a given day. You can be for sure he'll have a conversation with you.

CPSIA information can be obtained
at www.ICGtesting.com
Printed in the USA
BVHW091038140119
537773BV00021B/1585/P